The Instructor's Handbook

A PONY CLUB PUBLICATION

© The Pony Club 1993
  First Edition 1955
  Second Edition 1961
  Third Edition 1964
  Fourth Edition 1968
  Reprinted 1983 with the revised 'Standards of Efficiency'
  Fifth Edition 1985
  Reprinted 1989
  Reprinted 1991
  First paperback edition (updated), 1993
  Reprinted 1996, 2000
Designed by Alan Hamp
Diagrams by Victor Shreeve
Cover photograph by Bob Langrish
Illustrations by Joy Hawken

British Library Cataloguing in Publication Data
A catalogue record for this book is available from the British Library

Produced for The Pony Club by Barbara Cooper
Printed in Great Britain by Westway Offset, Wembley

ISBN 0-9537167-6-7

Preface

This book is designed primarily to encourage those who lack experience in how to teach, and to refresh the memories of those who do not teach on a regular basis. It should be used in conjunction with the Pony Club's official textbooks: *The Manual of Horsemanship, Keeping a Pony at Grass,* and *Breeding, Backing and Bringing On Young Horses and Ponies.* The *Instructors Folder*, containing the Pony Club Standards of Efficiency, is another useful guide.

Learning from a book can never be a substitute for attending Instructors' Courses and for experience gained while taking a ride, but these pages are intended to help Instructors to clarify their ideas and to teach with confidence, developing their own style within the suggested guidelines.

We hope that the book will be inspiring and helpful to everyone who instructs for the Pony Club.

Contents

FURTHER SUBJECTS FOR INSTRUCTION

FOR THE MORE EXPERIENCED INSTRUCTOR

APPENDIX
The Syllabus of Instruction for The Pony Club

Index

The Basics of Pony Club Instruction

1   General Principles

Working rallies are the backbone of the Pony Club. If they are enjoyable, young people will come to them and will benefit from what they are able to learn. The success of working rallies, therefore, depends on our Instructors.

No one can be forced to learn; there must be a desire to do so. Young people will only learn if there is an incentive, if the lesson is presented in an interesting way and if they can understand the reason for what they are doing.

The Qualities of a Good Instructor
- Genuine liking for young people, horses and ponies, and a desire to help them.
- An alert and enthusiastic personality.
- Self-confidence, which gives the ride a feeling of security.
- Powers of observation which, when developed, will quickly spot and correct basic faults.
- A clear, carrying voice which is easy to listen to.

Potential Instructors develop their ability by:
1. Gaining a thorough knowledge of Pony Club methods as outlined in *The Manual of Horsemanship*.
2. Studying the methods of more experienced Instructors.
3. Attending Instructors' courses.
4. Plenty of practice, combined with self-analysis.

Preparation Before the Rally
The success of any lesson depends largely on how well it has been prepared.
- It is important to know how many will be in the ride, their ages, and their ability. You should also be aware of the facilities and the amount of time available.
- The Chief Instructor should tell you which stage the ride has reached in the Pony Club syllabus. This will help you to decide what should be taught next.
- Work out the object of your lesson; know what you are aiming to achieve.
- Make an outline plan, such as:
    1. Inspection
    2. Working in

3. Revision
4. Explanation and demonstration of new subject to be taught (or 'lesson of the day')
5. Practice and corrections
6. Games

- Prepare the 'lesson of the day' thoroughly, producing points in a logical order, which will make them easier to understand and to remember.
- Study the syllabus. Read the text book. Know your subject matter *thoroughly*, so that you can explain it *clearly*.
- Try to develop your own way of making the lesson memorable and enjoyable.
- Prepare notes if it will help you, but do not read your lesson out, as this would be dull for your ride.
- Decide what props you will need, depending on your lesson plan and which games you will use.
- Decide whether you will need an assistant and/or a horse. Make the necessary arrangements.
- When teaching with video or films, make sure that either you or your assistant are familiar with the equipment and are able to use it correctly.
- Be prepared to adapt your lesson; circumstances can change in the best administrations.
- Teach a little, well.
- Plan to keep your ride SAFE, HAPPY AND ALERT.

Principles of Good Riding Instruction
- Be well turned out. You and your horse (if you are mounted) should be an example to your ride.
- Arrive early. Have enough time to adapt to last-minute changes. Check the area allocated to you. Organise props, and brief your assistant.
- Establish a rapport with every member of the ride.
- Keep up the interest of the ride; keep them active and alert. AVOID TOO MUCH TALKING.
- Speak clearly. Be simple and definite.
- Be quick to observe the basic faults, and be understanding in correcting them.
- Praise even the slightest improvement.
- Have an enquiring, open mind. Try to find out why a rider, horse, or pony is experiencing a particular difficulty.
- Keep order but do not bully. Never be sarcastic.

- Be firm but sympathetic, especially with nervous riders.
- Keep your eyes on the whole ride.
- Avoid spending too much time with one individual; the others will become bored. Try to give all riders an equal amount of attention.
- Use the affirmative *'Do'* rather than *'Don't'*: e.g., *'Carry your hands higher'*, not *'Don't carry your hands so low'*.
- When making an individual correction, say the name before the correction, e.g., *'Jane . . . look up'*.
- When asking questions, say the name last, e.g., *'What is a skewbald horse . . . Mary?'* This makes the whole ride think of the answer.
- Confirm by practical tests and questions that your ride has mastered each stage of the lesson.
- Try to find the reason for any disruptive behaviour, and act accordingly.
- Never be destructive. After criticism be sure to rebuilt confidence.
- Be cheerful and encouraging, ready to laugh at silly mishaps. Try to create in your ride the will to persevere.
- Know when to stop the working part of the lesson. Always end on a satisfactory note.
- Remember that the best riders and teachers strive for perfection. They will seldom reach it, but they must never give up trying.

Whether to instruct mounted or dismounted

Instructing dismounted is more sensible when teaching junior rides. It is safer, and the closer human contact gives the riders more confidence. Demonstrate by one of the following methods:
1. Use the most competent member of the ride.
2. Use a mounted assistant, perhaps a Junior Instructor.
3. Give a mini-demonstration yourself, on foot.
4. Ride a suitable pony borrowed out of the ride.
Demonstrations should be as polished and correct as possible unless they are being used deliberately to show faults.

Instructing while mounted is essential when taking the ride out on hacks. It is often preferable with more competent rides because:
1. You can give your own demonstrations and can illustrate faults.
2. If your horse is suitable, you might let certain members ride him in order to feel his movement.
3. You will have more scope in controlling your ride:
   a) When giving a cross-country lesson.
   b) When working the ride in a large area.
   c) While moving the ride from one place to another.

Before teaching while mounted consider the following:
1. Is the ride likely to be under reasonable control?
2. Is your position good enough to be a worthy example to your ride? Members copy their Instructors, but are quick to note their faults.
3. Will your horse stand patiently for long periods so that you can devote your whole attention to the ride?
4. If the manège is enclosed will it be large enough to accommodate the ride as well as a mounted Instructor?

FIRST AID

It is recommended that all Instructors should know the current BHS first aid procedure. If possible, they should hold the Red Cross/St John Ambulance Brigade First Aid Certificate.

In the event of an accident, the Instructor should immediately halt the ride, keep calm, and use his common sense. If necessary, he should send for help. Once first aid has been applied, and if circumstances permit, the Instructor should reassure the ride and continue his lesson.

Members who in the opinion of the Instructor have been or might have been concussed, must not ride again on the same day.

All accidents must be recorded in the Branch Accident Book.

2 Various Activities and Forms of Instruction

The responsibility for a branch's overall plan of instruction should stem from the branch Chief Instructor. He may or may not also be the District Commissioner. The plan of instruction should be based on the *Syllabus of Instruction for the Pony Club* (page 131). Suggestions for planning camps, day rallies and shorter afternoon or evening rallies are covered in *The District Commissioner's Handbook*.

Rallies are sometimes delegated to Rally Organisers who work in conjunction with the Chief Instructor.

At a rally, each ride should have a variety of activities and will probably move to different areas for each one of them. The Pony Club Instructor might be asked to take his ride for activities such as basic equitation, jumping, stable management and an instructional hack during the course of a day rally. Alternatively he could give one lesson at an evening rally.

The amount of guidance as to the content of the lessons will vary, but the Chief Instructor, sometimes working through the Rally Organiser, should arrange the timetable, allocate the facilities and notify those who will be teaching as to what type of lesson or lessons they will be asked to take (mounted, dismounted, large group, small group, etc.). He may also suggest or discuss with the Instructors what form the lessons should take. Whether mounted or dismounted, this will depend on:

☐ The facilities available.

☐ The size of the ride.

☐ The age and standard of the ride.

☐ The time available.

Below are some suggestions. Try to make the best of any given situation and, if necessary, modify your prepared lessons to make them safe and enjoyable for the standard of the ride.

NOTE: The ride should always be inspected before any mounted activity begins (see page 35).

FORMS OF INSTRUCTION–MOUNTED

THE CLASS LESSON

This is the most valuable way of teaching basic riding on the flat and over fences.

Suitable for: Up to 12 riders, but best for 5 to 8 riders.

Requirements: A flat area of at least 20 × 40 metres. A minimum of 4 markers, and either props for a game or a fence or two. Larger rides will need at least 20 × 60 metres, 4 corner markers, and 8 other markers (preferably letters). See pages 26 and 27 for diagrams of arenas.

Procedure: See page 34 for procedure, page 52 for jumping, or, where applicable, page 41 'Sample lessons for the very young'.

Over 12 riders: This is not recommended. It is difficult to achieve improvement with large numbers of riders in a class lesson. However, if it is unavoidable you should make sure that you know how to do interesting formation work and tricycling (see page 115).

The ride will become bored if worked in a dull routine with one rider following behind another. End the lesson with team games or jumping.

Up to 5 senior riders: The class lesson is essential for teaching more advanced riders, especially those working for 'A' Test who must be given concentrated and individual help. See page 125, 'Instructing Senior Rides'.

Up to 5 younger riders: Great progress can be made during a class lesson, but beware of overworking the ride. It is a challenge to make individual concentrated work enjoyable for the average or younger member. Plan to teach by means of carefully selected games. The lesson may be informal as small numbers are easier to control. See page 39, 'Instructing Beginners and the Very Young' and page 57, 'Teaching Riders to Jump'

INSTRUCTIONAL HACK OR COUNTRY RIDE

This is useful for teaching countryside studies, farming, and riding on the roads and through the countryside. The aim is to encourage members to ride with intelligence and consideration for others and to be aware of the pace used while hacking, in various conditions.

Suitable for: Any size ride, but particularly useful when large numbers have to be taken by one Instructor.

Requirements: A quiet horse for the Instructor to ride.

With junior rides, there should be one extra helper for every five children; competent Associates are ideal.

Several leading-reins.

Fluorescent warning strips or vests for the Instructor and assistants when riding on the road.

Procedure: You should have a competent rider in front, who knows the way and who will set a sensible pace. Position yourself or a helper at the back, where the whole ride can be watched and problems quickly noticed.

On the road:

Ride on the left in groups of three or four pairs.

The first pair of each group should be competent. Young ponies should be on the left of steady ponies.

Leave room for 2 or 3 cars to overtake between each group.

When crossing the road, unless the ride is very large, wait until everyone has caught up, turn, and cross as one unit. (See 'Road Safety', page 86.)

In open country:

Keep control. Do not canter unless the ride is settled and safe at a trot. For the first canter send the ride up a hill, one after another, stopping before they reach the top. Impetuous ponies should go first. (See 'Countryside Studies and Hunting', page 84.)

FORMATION RIDING

Suitable for:

Average or large size rides.

Requirements:

A flat area 20 × 40 metres, or 30 × 60 metres for larger rides.

Corner markers and letters.

If riding to music, a tape recorder and suitable tapes.

Procedure:

At first, practise each movement in walk without music. Always call the movements. (See page 118, 'Producing a Formation Ride'.)

MOCK HUNT

Suitable for:

Large numbers. This can be great fun for everyone and is suitable during an afternoon at a day rally or camp.

Requirements:

Permission from one or two farmers to ride through woodland and across or round some fields.

A carefully planned route marked appropriately with trails and false trails.

Sawdust, shavings or white, washable emulsion paint for laying the trails. Paper should not be used as it litters the countryside.

Plenty of mounted assistants and mobile back up help.

Procedure: An adult should be the huntsman. Appoint members to be whippers-in, hounds, field masters, gate shutters etc. Although the huntsman should know the route, it is more fun if he hunts the 'hounds' as realistically as possible, using his horn correctly, casting, and allowing 'hounds' to 'pick up the scent'. (See 'Countryside Studies and Hunting', page 84).

PAPER CHASE

This is not as instructive as the mock hunt, but is easier to prepare and can be over a shorter distance.

Suitable for: A large ride or several rides joining together. An enjoyable way to end a day rally.

Requirements: As for a mock hunt. See above.

Procedure: Members should work as individuals or in pairs.

SCAVENGER HUNT

This is useful for teaching the ride to identify trees and plants, or simply as a game.

Suitable for: Any size ride, but particularly useful for ending a lesson with large groups of younger children, perhaps working them in pairs.

Requirements: Either 'planted' items or natural items growing in the area.

Procedure: Define the boundaries. Explain that items must be searched for and collected from within the defined area. Name the items to be found. If they are plants or leaves, show examples and discuss the advantages and disadvantages of having them growing in a paddock. The degree of difficulty of the items chosen should be according to the standard of the ride. The very young should play the game only at walk or trot, and should collect items which do not entail dismounting.

GYMKHANA GAMES

These are useful for teaching the correct way of riding with the reins in one hand, mounting and dismounting from both sides at the halt, vaulting on and off while the ponies move forward, leading mounted and dismounted etc., or for recreation at the end of a rally.

Suitable for: Any size of ride, as long as you have enough props.

Requirements: Any gymkhana props. With 4 rows of bending poles, 4 buckets, 4 scarves and some paper cups, several games can be played.

If you are training the branch gymkhana team, have the appropriate props to be used in the games chosen for that year.

Procedure: Split the ride into teams, achieving a balance between the skilful and less competent riders. For ideas about games see the Pony Club book *Gymkhanas and Rally Games*.

DRESSAGE LESSON

Suitable for: Smaller rides. Best with fewer than 6 riders so that each one may have a chance to practise on his own in the arena.

Requirements: An accurately marked out dressage arena, 20 × 40 metres, with letters and corner markers.

Procedure: See diagram of arena, page 27 and 'Riding a Dressage Test', page 87.

SHOW-JUMPING LESSON

Suitable for: Average or smaller size rides.

Requirements: A course of show jumps on a flat piece of ground.

Procedure: See 'Show Jumping', page 90.

CROSS-COUNTRY LESSON

Suitable for: Any size of ride.

Requirements: A variety of cross-country fences.
A quiet horse for the Instructor if you decide to ride.
An assistant or two depending on the size and standard of the ride, either mounted, or in a cross-country vehicle (e.g. Land-Rover).

Procedure: With less experienced riders, the Instructor should be dismounted. (See 'Riding Across Country', page 94.)

ROAD SAFETY LESSON

Suitable for: Average or smaller size rides. Best with fewer than 9 riders.

Requirements: A flat area approx 100 × 60 metres. Markers and other equipment used in the Field Test layout of the current Riding and Road Safety Test.

Procedure: See 'Road Safety', page 86.

DISCUSSION

Suitable for: A break during any lesson, in a quiet, sheltered place.

Procedure: This can take place spontaneously, at any time, to give ponies and riders a rest. With the ponies standing in a semi-circle, choose a suitable topic, then start a discussion, encouraging everyone to join in. Five minutes will be ample. Do not allow the ride to get cold. (See the 'Five-minute Talk', page 78.)

FORMS OF INSTRUCTION – DISMOUNTED

PRACTICAL STABLE MANAGEMENT

This is the most constructive way to teach stable management, as members can be shown how something should be done and then practise doing it for themselves.

Suitable for:	Groups of up to 8 members.
Requirements:	Good-quality props or the use of a well-appointed stable yard, with, for example, tack in saddle room; samples of various feed-stuffs in feed room; hay and straw in hay barn; horse box; grooming kit; blacksmith's tools; a quiet pony, or members' own ponies.
Procedure:	If possible, the subject should be taught in its appropriate environment. For example, explain about 'feeding' in the feed room. You can then discuss storage and methods of feeding as well as identifying various feeds.
	It is important for everyone to do some practical work.
Smaller groups:	With fewer members you will have more time, so take the opportunity to cover the subject in greater detail. (See 'Horsemastership', page 74).

STABLE MANAGEMENT TASKS

This is a good way for members to learn or revise several aspects of practical stable management. Each group moves to each task point in turn.

Suitable for:	9 to 18 members.
Requirements:	Three task points such as:

1. Grooming point. Quiet pony correctly tied up; grooming kit.
2. Tack cleaning point. Sufficient tack cleaning equipment for everyone in a group; some dirty tack.
3. Saddling-up point. One or two quiet ponies correctly tied up; saddles and bridles to fit them. One Instructor or an assistant for each task point and pony.

Procedure:	Brief your assistant thoroughly. They must teach each group according to its standard.
	Make sure that they teach the reasons why it is important for the tasks to be done well: e.g., ponies soon become nervous at the sight

of their saddlery unless it is sympathetically put on.

Divide the members into groups of up to 6 of a similar standard.

Groups move to each task point, where after a brief demonstration members practise the task while their Instructor makes comments and gives advice. (See 'Horsemastership', page 74.)

TEXT BOOK – THE PONY CLUB MANUAL OF HORSEMANSHIP

Suitable for: Teaching horsemastership or theory of equitation to average or small size groups when no props are available.

Requirements: Somewhere comfortable to sit. Copies of the *Manual*.

Procedure: Each member of the group takes a turn in reading aloud from selected pages. When necessary make interventions to elaborate on or to demonstrate a particular point.

Stress the importance of reading as a means of learning.

VIDEO

Suitable for: Groups small enough to enable everyone to have a good view of the screen.

Requirements: Video equipment and, if possible, a camera. Preferably a room set aside for video viewing, with a TV screen which can be easily seen by the class while sitting comfortably.

Suitable cassettes or video recordings of the ride taken during a recent lesson.

Procedure: See 'Using Video', page 80.

THE QUIZ

Suitable for: Groups of any size. The gathering may be on a large scale (involving other branches, for example) when it will require considerable preparation; or it may merely be used as a way of helping a small group to learn a subject perhaps after lunch at a rally.

Requirements:	A place suitable for the type and size of the gathering and for the length of the quiz.
Procedure:	If you are using the quiz to teach 5 or 12 members at a rally or camp, form teams. Either ask the questions yourself, or arrange for everyone to read the appropriate pages of the *Manual* beforehand, and instruct each one to produce 2 questions to ask the opposing team. You could also use the *Pony Club Quiz Book.*

THE LECTURE

Suitable for:	Groups of any size. Particularly useful when teaching large numbers.
Requirements:	A comfortable, quiet place where the group can sit. Visual aids.
Procedure:	See 'Giving a Lecture', page 78.

DISCUSSION

Suitable for:	Any group at any time.
Procedure:	Spontaneous discussions are appropriate, either during stable management sessions out of doors, or in the class room. Give a short introduction, then start a discussion, perhaps by asking an individual 'How do you do this?' Discussion keeps everyone on their toes; they must all be encouraged to join in. See 'The Five-minute Talk', page 78.

3 Use of the Voice

The ride should be able to hear the Instructor clearly and without effort. Most men and a large percentage of women can be easily heard. A few Instructors have great difficulty in 'throwing' their voice and suffer very considerable stress after an hour or so of teaching. They are advised to seek professional help from a voice production teacher.

In order to ensure that you are heard clearly, the following points may be helpful:

- Position yourself with the ride in front of you. When out of doors, have your back to the wind.
- Look up.
- Don't shout.
- Use your lips, the tip of your tongue and your jaw actively to produce good vowel and consonant sounds.
- Speak more slowly than you normally do.
- Vary the tone and speed of your voice, to add expression and enthusiasm.
- Don't let your voice die away at the end of the sentence (this is usually due to lack of breath).
- Don't be afraid of silence. Use it! A pause is often better than repeating yourself.
- Try to relax your throat and the muscles at the back of your tongue.
- ABOVE ALL TRY TO BREATHE CORRECTLY. This requires some practice.

First, take an especially deep breath and hold it ... you will almost certainly have produced a total block in your throat. When you let go, your breath will rush out. This is incorrect. Instead, place your hands on either side of the ribs nearest to your waistband. Breathe slowly in, first filling the space between your hands, then letting your chest fill with air. Finally, without allowing that 'block' to happen, continue breathing out gently and smoothly, until your ribs squeeze out the last of the air, and your hands move inwards.

Do not worry if after two or three such breaths you feel dizzy or have to cough. It just means that you are using a part of your lungs that haven't been used for some time.

Good breathing produces a well-controlled voice which will carry.

Taking The
Mounted Ride

4 Controlling the Ride During a Class Lesson

It is of vital importance for the Instructor to be confident and familiar with the simple terms of command. He will thus be at ease when controlling the ride.

The riding area (Figs, 1, 2, 3, 4).
A ride is more easily controlled in an arena or manège (or school).

The four corners should be clearly marked, ideally with boards, otherwise with cones.

It is helpful if centre, 'quarter', and half markers are correctly lettered. For competitions the centre lines, and letters D, X, G, etc, are generally marked by mowing. They are not normally marked at rallies.

If you are using an arena without letters or have merely been allocated a space in a field, use any safe objects, such as cones, or buckets with the handles removed.

Corner markers are the first priority, followed by centre, 'quarter', and half markers.

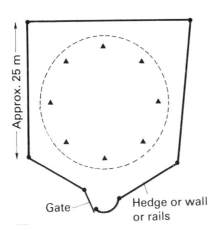

Gate — Hedge or wall or rails

Fig. 1 Small enclosed area suitable for beginners or the very young. The track is outside the markers.

Fig. 2 Large arena suitable for rides of over 12 members and for formation riding. Here marked with upturned buckets or cones.

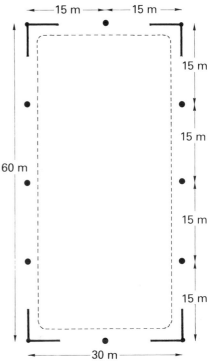

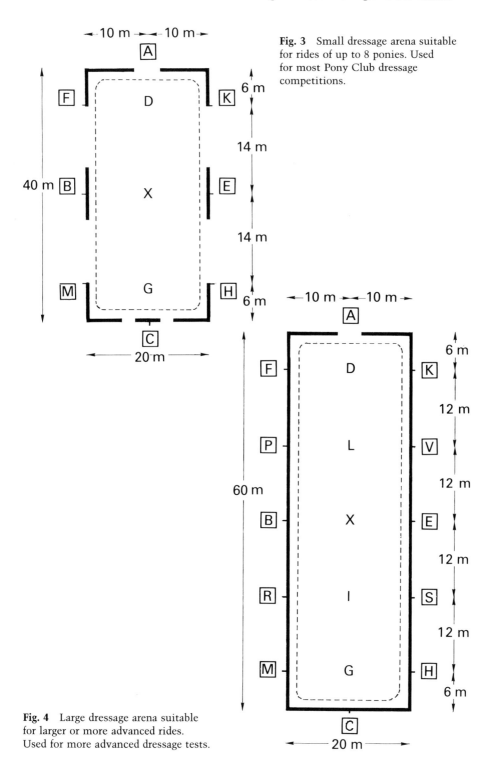

Fig. 3 Small dressage arena suitable for rides of up to 8 ponies. Used for most Pony Club dressage competitions.

Fig. 4 Large dressage arena suitable for larger or more advanced rides. Used for more advanced dressage tests.

Order of Riding
Members of the ride normally ride one behind the other – that is in single file.
The rider at the front is called 'leading file'.
The rider at the back is called 'rear file'.
PACE (OR GAIT) This should change only when the command is given.
SPEED The leading file sets the speed. An even, steady, regular pace should be maintained as far as possible by all ride members.
DISTANCE Riders are responsible for maintaining the distance between their own ponies and the heels of the pony in front. The distance is usually half a horse's length (approx. 1.5 metres or 5ft), but this may be varied to suit circumstances and safety.
TRACKS The outer track is just within the perimeter of the manège. The ride should stay on this track, riding the corners as quarter circles, unless told to do otherwise.
   The inner track should be ridden 1.5 metres inside the outer track.
DIRECTION   *'On the right rein'* means clockwise.
            'On the left rein' means anti-clockwise.
            'Track right' means turn to the right on reaching the track.
            'Track left' means turn to the left on reaching the track.
SIMPLE SCHOOL MOVEMENTS
Circles Changes of rein* Turns* Loops* Serpentines*.
*These are described with words of command and diagrams under 'Sample Turns and Changes of Rein (Direction)' on page 30.

Directive Terms
'Whole ride' means all together.
'In succession' means one at a time.
'Walk on a loose rein' means gradually lengthen the reins, allowing the pony to stretch his neck forwards and down.
'Make much of your ponies' means give your ponies a rewarding pat.
'Sit at ease' means lengthen the reins so that the pony can rest while at halt.
'Go large' means return to the outer track and remain on the same rein.

Position of the Instructor
Ideally, the Instructor should place himself with his back to the wind and about 2 metres (6½ft) from the track and from the centre line. From here he can watch the ride easily and will not interfere with movements, such as turns down the centre or changes of rein. He should, however, feel free to move in order to observe riders or ponies from different angles.

WORDS OF COMMAND

Words of command have three functions:
1. WHO is being given the command: e.g., *'Whole ride'*, *'In succession'*, or the rider's name, etc.
2. WHAT they are commanded to do: e.g., *'Prepare to trot'*.
3. WHEN the command must be carried out: e.g., *'Ride ter – rot'*, or *'Leading file commence'*
   OR
4. WHERE the command must be carried out: e.g. *'At the H marker'* or *'As you cross the centre line'*. Thus the riders will know that they must *either* 'do it now' (3) or 'do it later at the named place' (4).

Examples
'Whole ride, prepare to trot' ... (pause) ... *'Ride ter – rot'*.
'In succession, turn down the centre line and halt at X, then rejoin the rear of the ride' ... (pause ... *'Leading file commence'* ... (and then) ... *'Next'*, *'Next'*, etc.

Time your commands and speak them clearly, pausing between each stage. Give the executive command (e.g., *'Leading file commence'*) when the rider has arrived at a good place to begin the exercise.

If you begin your commands too late, the riders will not have enough time to prepare, and may pass the point where the exercise is to be performed. It is better to begin too early and then pause for a few seconds before giving the final command.

The ride should act on the executive command accurately and smoothly. If the executive word is drawn out ('ter – rot') rather than snapped ('trot'), good transitions will be encouraged. The tone of your voice will influence ponies and riders. The increase of pace should be on an upward note, and the decrease of pace on a falling note.

ALWAYS MAKE SURE THAT THE RIDERS UNDERSTAND THE WORDS OF COMMAND.
That they know their left from their right.
That your leading file is competent and preferably has done school work before.

Commanding School Movements
The following terms may be used if letters are not available:
'Centre markers' for A and C.
'Quarter markers' for F, K, H and M.
'Half markers' for B and E.
CIRCLES may be ridden in single file or in succession. Generally a 20-metre circle is a good size. Smaller circles can be asked for and their size carefully explained.

Sample Turns and Changes of Rein (Direction)
'In single file, at E turn right, at B track left' (Fig. 5a)
OR
'In single file, at E turn right, at B track right' (to stay on the same rein Fig. 5b).

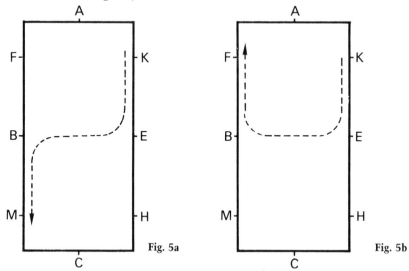

Fig. 5a   Fig. 5b

'In single file, at C turn down the centre line, at A track right'
(Fig. 6a).
OR
'In single file, at C turn down the centre line, at A track left' (to stay on the same rein Fig. 6b).

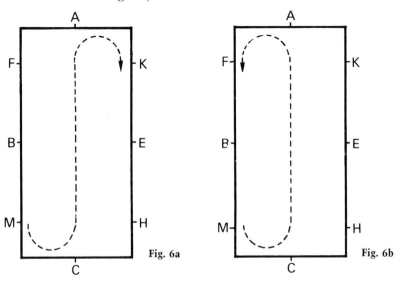

Fig. 6a   Fig. 6b

'In single file, right (or inwards) incline to change the rein from K'
(Fig. 7).

'In single file, at A half-circle right to X and half-circle left to C' (Fig. 8).

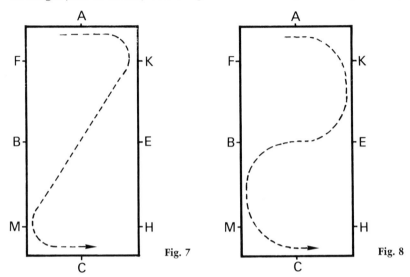

Fig. 7

Fig. 8

'In single file, ride a loop of 5 metres between F and M' (Fig. 9).
'In single file, ride a serpentine of three large loops from A to C, each
loop touching the track' (Fig. 10).

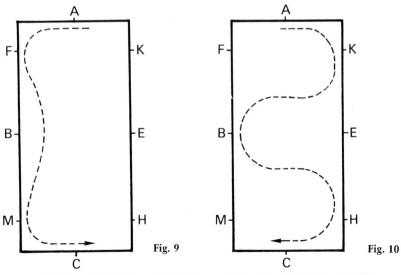

Fig. 9

Fig. 10

AVOID ENDLESS TROTTING ROUND THE MANEGE

TO HALT AND TO MOVE OFF

(Please note that the diagrams are not drawn to scale)

The simplest and the most expedient method in an emergency
'Whole ride, prepare to halt, ride ha—alt.'
'Whole ride, prepare to walk, walk on'.

Useful when talking or demonstrating to the ride

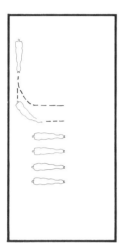

'Leading file, at M (or other named marker) inwards turn and halt, the remainder form a ride on his left (or right)'
(Fig. 11a).

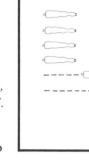

'In succession, from the right, walk and track left; walk on'.
(Fig. 11b).

Fig. 11a   **Fig. 11b**

The easiest halt for the ponies
'Leading file prepare to halt; the remainder turn in and form a ride on his left (or right); leading file ha—alt'. (Fig. 12a).
'In succession, from the right (or left), prepare to walk and track left (or right); walk on'. (Fig. 12b).

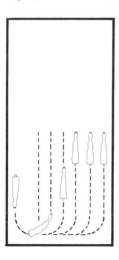

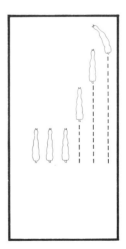

Fig. 12a   **Fig. 12b**

To halt, keeping the ponies well apart
'*Whole ride pepare to run in and halt 3 metres in from the track; ride turn*'. (Fig. 13a).
'*Whole ride, prepare to walk and track right (or left); walk on*'. (Fig. 13b).

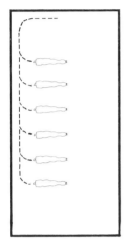

Fig. 13a

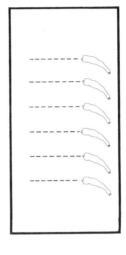

Fig. 13b

Before halting the ride, consider:
- ☐ If you are going to do a demonstration, will they be able to see?
- ☐ Will there be sufficient room in front of them?
- ☐ Will the sun be shining directly in their or your eyes?
- ☐ Can you use hedges or buildings as shelter from the elements?

SCHOOL MANNERS AND DISCIPLINE

Throughout the lesson the ride remains:
- ☐ In single file.
- ☐ On the outer track.
- ☐ On the same rein.
- ☐ The same distance apart.
- ☐ In the basic paces (medium walk, working trot and working canter) until commanded otherwise.

- • After completing a commanded movement, the rider should return to the outer track.
- • If the distance between two riders becomes too great, the rider who is left behind should cut the manège short by turning early across the short side. The riders behind him should follow.
- • Riders should sit on the correct diagonal.

- When moving in opposite directions, riders must pass left hand to left hand.
- Whips are generally carried in the inside hand. When using a whip, care should be taken to avoid upsetting another rider's pony.
- Tongue-clicking should be discouraged.
- Consideration should be shown to other members of the ride, and riders should be taught to be attentive to the behaviour of other ponies and to act accordingly.
- The Instructor should always encourage good manners in his ride.

The above terms and disciplines are a simple means of controlling a ride safely and effectively. The Instructor who is conversant with them will be free to apply himself to the more important task of teaching.

For more ambitious ways of controlling the ride, see 'School Movements performed in various ways – formation riding'. (Page 100).

5   Procedure for Giving a Class Lesson

Before you begin you should:
- [ ] Prepare your lesson according to the information given to you in advance. (In some Branches, you will be asked to teach a certain subject; in others it will be left to your discretion).
- [ ] Inspect the area where you will be teaching.
- [ ] Check your 'props'.
- [ ] Brief your assistant (if you have one).

When taking the ride you should bear in mind the following points:
1. Try to develop good communication by asking frequent questions and by encouraging questions and comments from the ride.
2. Choose with care the time when you reach your 'lesson of the day'.
3. Members and their ponies tire quickly; therefore both need frequent periods of rest, with ponies walking on a loose rein or riders 'sitting at ease'.
4. Concentration lasts for short periods only. It must be constantly re-stimulated.
5. Emphasis should vary between physical effort, mental effort, excitement, and relaxation.

You might use the following outline on which to base a rally period of two hours. Because of the time taken during the preliminaries and moving to your area and back, your working time will probably be one and a half hours.

Introduction and Inspection

As a rule the Rally Organiser will allocate your ride and introduce the members to you. Before moving off, make sure that they know your name. Line them up, and make your inspection in a place where help, spare equipment, leather-punch, numnahs etc, are close at hand.

With each rider:

- Establish a friendly rapport while you quickly make your checks.
- Ask each member his name and the name and age of his horse or pony.
- Find out if the animal is owned, borrowed, or hired, and if he kicks or has any other problems.
- Note the condition of the horse/pony. If he is very thin or dull, tactfully find out why. Refer any completely unsuitable animals to the DC or Rally Organiser, who should advise the parents.
- Make sure that every rider on a young horse or pony has a neckstrap. (For details on fitting the neckstrap, see page 39).
- Check that the rider's hat and footwear comply with the current official safety rules. Riders with unsuitable footwear should ride without stirrups.

Then:

- Check the fit and condition of saddlery. Members should not be allowed to ride with:
1. Stirrups which are much too small (the foot can wedge) or much too large (the heel can slide through). A rider may be allowed to join in without stirrup-irons and leathers.
2. Stirrup leathers, girths or reins with rotten leather or stitching.
3. Girths which are too loose when on the tightest holes.
- As temporary measures, fit numnahs to saddles which are too low, and knot reins which are too long. (Make a knot at the buckle end).
- Explain that saddlery must fit correctly because no horse or pony will work properly if he is uncomfortable. As he carries his rider's weight through the saddle, its fit is, obviously, vital. Bridles can also cause discomfort: e.g. tight browbands pinch the base of the ears; tight throat-lashes become too restrictive when the pony tries to relax his jaw; bits which are too big have incorrect actions.
- Be aware that the rider will have difficulty in sitting correctly in a saddle which tips him too far forward, or (more common) too far back. (A good saddler can make adjustments.)
- Remember that you are there to help and teach, not to judge and

condemn. Correct that which is dangerous or uncomfortable, make necessary adjustments, and suggest that any lesser problems should be put right by the next rally.

- Always praise those who are well turned out.
- Refer dangerous and unsolvable problems to the DC or Rally Organiser.
- Arrange your ride in pairs, with keen ponies in front and kickers at the back. Lead them to your area at the walk.

THE RIDING AREA is described on page 26. It should be preferably be on flat, well-drained land.

CONTROLLING THE RIDE: Chapter 4 covers the minimum requirements. Make sure that you know where to stand and what to say. When you are more experienced and can control your ride with ease and confidence, see Chapter 18, 'School Movements Performed in Various Ways – Formation Riding', page 100.

Working-in the Ride

Line up your riders side by side, facing you, with half a horse's length between them. Tell them briefly what you plan to do during the lesson.

Make sure that they check their girths and remind them to re-check after a short period of work.

See that they know the commands and expressions which you will use to control them, and that they know their left from their right.

Work the ride on both reins at walk and trot.

Observe each horse/pony and rider carefully and form an opinion of them.

At this stage make few comments. *GIVE THEM TIME TO SETTLE DOWN.*

Check that your leading file sets a good constant pace.

Change the ride order if necessary.

Use simple school movements to help the ride to supple up.

Avoid small circles and complicated movements.

As soon as they have settled down and you have made your assessment, halt the ride.

Basic Corrections

Explain the importance of the correct position, and adjust the length of stirrup leathers if necessary. At all times the Instructor should be aware of each rider's faults and should make corrections where necessary, constantly encouraging the rider to work on his position. (See 'The Rider's Position', page 45).

Revise The aids, re-affirming previous lessons.

Physical Exercises
If the ponies are calm and obedient, use physical exercises to help the riders' balance and to increase their confidence. See page 48.

THE LESSON OF THE DAY

The right time to begin teaching your subject is about twenty minutes after the beginning of the lesson. By now the riders and ponies should be well settled down and ready to concentrate on your lesson, which should follow these basic principles:

1. **Plan**
   This should be part of your advance preparation. It should include knowledge of numbers, age group, standard, and what the Branch Chief Instructor requires.
2. **Explanation**
   What your are going to teach and why.
3. **Demonstration**
   This should show clearly *how* to do whatever you are teaching, and can be demonstrated by you, your assistant, or a ride member.
4. **Practice**
   The rides puts into practice what has been explained and demonstrated, completing the sequence of HEAR, SEE, FEEL. Practice might be carried out individually, as a ride, or in groups, depending on the movement and the space available.
5. **Correction**
   You should comment with praise or corrections as and when you see it happening.
6. **Re-demonstrate**
   They may find it helpful to be shown again.
7. **Practise again**
8. **Comment again**
9. **Questions**
   Confirm by questioning that they have fully understood the lesson. Be tactful with those who need further explanation.

The lesson of the day does not have to be on the flat but could well be jumping or a related subject such as 'the approach to a fence', or 'riding a track'.

During this period the maximum time should be spent by the ride *doing*, and the minimum time by the Instructor talking and demonstrating.

Be quick to observe the good or the not so good, and comment on them accordingly. If you can give the rider the 'feel' of what is correct, you will have taught a good lesson.

Period of Relaxation

After the period of concentration or exertion there should be a short break, when you can discuss an item of interest (e.g. 'Do you all know the name of your pony's bit and what it is made of?'), or play a quiet game (e.g. equestrian items beginning with certain letters of the alphabet). (See 'The Five-Minute Talk', page 78.)

Jumping

Most members will feel deprived if there is no jumping at a rally, but occasionally there may be children who don't enjoy it. Be aware of this minority and do not force or frighten them.

Jumping may take many forms and can be related to the lesson of the day. Some suggestions are:

- ☐ The single fence.
- ☐ The double or treble fence.
- ☐ A course of jumps.
- ☐ A cross-country ride including natural fences.
- ☐ Cross-country fences.
- ☐ Jumping up and down hill.
- ☐ Ditches.
- ☐ Jumping without stirrups.

This is also a good opportunity to explain how to put up safe jumps at home. For more detailed ideas see 'Jumping Exercises using a small amount of equipment' page 66).

Games

Depending on the time available, how much work the ponies have done, and how tired the riders are, it can be fun to play a game. Even quite senior riders enjoy this; the ponies certainly do. It is a good idea to relate the game to the lesson which you have taught, e.g.:

- ☐ TURNS AND CIRCLES Bending
- ☐ MOUNTING AND DISMOUNTING Musical Sacks
- ☐ THE APPROACH TO A FENCE   The stride game. (The rider counts backwards during the approach to a fence.) See page 69.
- ☐ ALTERING STIRRUPS   A team race. Start at normal length, ride to far end, shorten stirrup leathers, and return over small jumps.
- ☐ CROSS-COUNTRY RIDE   'I spy', with flora and fauna.

Use your own ingenuity to add to these ideas.

Ending the Lesson
It is important for the ponies to be cool by the end of the lesson, as they may be travelling home by box, or standing tied up for the next part of the rally.

Spend the final few minutes re-affirming the important lessons learned and reminding each individual of the things they must remember and practise before the next rally.

Give back any whips or other items which you have taken from the riders. Make sure that any borrowed numnahs etc, are returned.

Walk the ride safely back to 'base', and report progress to the DC or Rally Organiser.

Reflection
Lastly, make a mental or written note of how successful the rally was and how it might have been improved. Everyone makes mistakes. Try to learn from both the good and the less successful parts of your programme.

6   Instructing Beginners and the Very Young

EXTRA ITEMS WHICH WILL BE REQUIRED

Neckstraps Every beginner should have one of these. Either a narrow stirrup leather or a shortened martingale strap is best. Fit the neckstrap so that it rests one-third of the way up the pony's neck where the rider can hold it in an emergency or, later, when learning to jump. A piece of string may be fitted from the front 'D' on the saddle to the neckstrap, to prevent it from slipping forward if the pony lowers his head. Make sure that borrowed neckstraps are returned to you after the rally.

String to make grass-reins Grass-reins prevent a pony from grazing while being ridden. There are various ways of fitting them. Two ways are:
1. Run a piece of string from the front 'D' of the saddle through the back of the noseband and back to the 'D' on the other side.
2. Run two pieces of string from the front 'D' of the saddle down through the loop of the browband to the ring of the bit. The pony must be free to use his head and neck. Fit the grass-reins so that he

can stretch his nose to within at least 18 ins., (46cm) of the ground but is not able to try and eat the grass.

Props for games Make sure that you have a supply of cones or safe markers and other items that you will need to play the games you have planned.

EXTRA SADDLERY TO BE CHECKED
As well as the normal inspection described on page 35, check:
1. STIRRUP BARS in the form of a fixed 'D'. When stirrup leathers are attached through a fixed 'D' (often found on felt saddles) *safety stirrups must be used.*
2. REINS These should be narrow to fit children with small fingers.

Special Considerations when Taking the Ride:
- Remember that these young and inexperienced riders must not be frightened; are unable to concentrate for long; and must enjoy themselves – learning through games. SAFETY is a prime consideration.
- The Instructor should be dismounted.
- An enclosed area is essential (see Fig. 1 on page 26.) Check that the gate is shut.
- Make the manège approx. 25 × 25 metres, or adaptable to the number of riders and the size of their animals.
- Some of the ponies may be on leading-reins. In any case, have plenty of competent dismounted assistants.
- Work the ride on the outside of the markers as this will make the track a better shape and will stop the ponies cutting in.
- If numbers are few, it is sometimes easier to halt the ride on the track in single file rather than facing inwards.
- The first priority is to help each rider to feel confident, happy with his pony and 'at home' on his pony's back.

Keep the working-in period short, and then correct the riders' positions, adjusting stirrup leather lengths if necessary.

All beginners feel more secure with slightly short leathers. But do not allow them to ride on the backs of their saddles.

Those who have difficulty in holding their reins at the correct length can sometimes be helped by marking with rubber bands the places where each hand should be.

The lesson of the day should be simple and easily remembered. (Examples follow.)

To practise what you have taught, get the ride moving as soon as possible. Then play a few carefully selected games which incorporate what you have been teaching. The games need not be competitive as not all children want to compete at this stage.

SAMPLE LESSONS

The following sample lessons are intended for members aged 6 to 11, but may be adapted for older, inexperienced members. The lessons are progressive.

MOVING OFF AND STOPPING
Suitable for a pre-D ride on or off the leading-rein. You should be dismounted, but borrow a demonstrator, perhaps from a more experienced ride. The stages (pre-D, D1 and D2) are described on pages 132–3.
1. **Plan** your lesson bearing the age of the riders in mind, and also the devious behaviour of some of the ponies.
2. **Explain** After inspecting the ride and working-in, line up the riders and tell them that today you are going to teach them how to move off and halt correctly, which will make it easier for them to control their ponies; ponies are more obedient when they are given clear aids.
3. **Demonstrate** (a) Preparing to walk.
                   (b) How some ponies will move from a very light aid.
                   (c) What to do if a stronger aid is needed.
                   (d) How to guide the pony.
                   (e) How to stop with the minimum of fuss.
4. **Practise** From where they are standing as a ride, they should prepare to walk, and walk forward in succession. You can then make a comment to each one. Once on the track, in single file, they can practise halting and moving off as a ride. Later they might practise in pairs or with the whole ride abreast up the length of the school.
5. **Correct** Praise or correct at the relevant moment. Always be encouraging.
6. **Re-affirm** by playing some games, such as 'Simon says' or 'Grandmother's footsteps', which involve moving off and halting. End the game by demonstrating correctly the smooth way to move off and halt.

TURNS AND CIRCLES
Suitable for a pre-D standard ride, on or off the leading-rein. Be dismounted and, if possible, have a mounted assistant, perhaps a Junior Instructor. You will need a few small bean poles or any safe markers.
1. **Plan** the whole lesson beforehand.

2. ***Explain*** After inspecting the ride and working-in, line up the riders and tell them that today they will learn to turn their ponies correctly and that they will use markers to help them. If you have enough helpers to hold the ponies, let the ride dismount and help you to set out pairs of markers to make a path on a straight line, round a half-circle (about 5 metres in diameter) and back down a straight line (Fig. 14).

Let the ride run down the track on foot. Tell them to look where they are going.

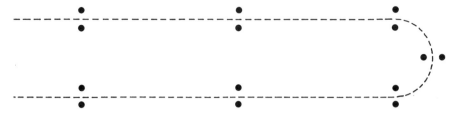

Fig. 14 'The Path.'

3. ***Demonstrate*** how a pony should walk down the path, round the corner, and back again, looking where *he* is going. Show how the rider should use his legs to keep the pony on the path along the straight parts and should use an open rein while turning.

4. ***Practise***, perhaps by playing a game called 'Hannibal' in which the path is a narrow mountain track. Anyone who knocks down a marker has fallen off the track and must start again. With the demonstrator (e.g. Hannibal) as leading file the ride should, at first, go round the outer track, and then along the marked path. Change the rein. Insist on correct distances between each pony throughout the exercise.

5. ***Correct*** when necessary, but always be encouraging.

6. ***Re-demonstrate*** in the form of a game. The demonstrator makes deliberate mistakes, such as showing what happens if the rider pulls too much on one rein. Members of the ride spot the mistakes and correct them. Then demonstrate the correct way to turn.

7. ***Play a team game***. For example, divide the ride into two teams, each with its own 'Hannibal'. While one team practises the exercise, as (4) above, on one rein, the other team watches and makes comments. Next the second team performs while the first team watches. Then in turn, they both do the exercise on the other rein. Award marks, or have some way of making the game exciting. The winning team is the one which gets to the 'top of the mountain' with fewest casualties.

RISING TROT
Suitable for a stage pre-D or D1 Ride. Be dismounted, but have a mounted demonstrator, perhaps one member of the ride who is more advanced and can do a reasonable rising trot. It is helpful to have a few dismounted assistants.
1. **Plan** your lesson according to the age and standard of the ride.
2. After inspecting the ride and working-in, line up the riders, and by asking questions such as 'Has your pony got a bumpy trot?' or 'How do you feel when he is trotting?' *explain* rising trot. Tell them that they are going to perform some rising and some sitting trot.
3. **Demonstrate**   (a) How to ask the pony to trot.
    (b) Sitting trot.
    (c) Rising trot.
Explain that rising trot is more comfortable for the pony and the rider, especially when riding long distances. During the demonstration tell them to call 'One-two, one-two . . .' in time with the sitting trot, and 'Up-down, up-down . . .' in time with the rising trot.
4. At the halt, let the ride *practise* 'going up-down' (forward and down to help them to stay in balance) in the rhythm of the trot. Some riders may need to hold their neckstraps.
5. While the ride walks round the school, the leading file trots down the long side, showing a few strides of sitting trot and then rising. The less experienced should be led by an assistant, who should watch the rider and be ready to steady him if necessary.
6. **Make corrections** and give plenty of encouragement.
7. **Play a game** – for example, a relay, which need not be a race. Divide the ride into 2 teams. One member of each team walks to a marker, turns around it, and comes back at rising trot. As he reaches the team, the next one starts, and so on.
    Once the ride is confident at rising trot, give a lesson on diagonals.
    Mark one diagonal pair of legs on the demonstrator's pony, using ribbons or bandages of the same colour: it is then easier for the ride to see how the legs move.

TRANSITION TO CANTER
Suitable for a D2 standard ride. Either give your own demonstrations or bring in a demonstrator, perhaps borrowed from a more experienced ride. To help the ride to see how the legs move, use three differently coloured bandages. The left canter will be clearly seen if the horse's legs are marked as follows: near-fore colour 1; off-fore and near hind colour 2; off-hind colour 3.

1. **Plan** the lesson, referring to the *Manual of Horsemanship*. Keep it simple.
2. After inspecting the riders and working-in, line them up at one end of the manège and teach your main subject or 'lesson of the day', first *explaining* that this will show how the pony canters; the aids for the transition to canter; and how the rider should sit.
3. **Demonstrate the canter and the transitions** on a large circle at the far end of the manège. Ask questions like 'Which foreleg is leading?', to make the ride watch carefully, and learn by watching. Show the canter on the other rein. Confirm that the canter is in three beats, with the inside foreleg leading.

Emphasize the following: (a) The previous pace.
    (b) The easiest place to make the transition.
    (c) The aids.
    (d) The position of the rider's body.

4. **Practise**. Move the ride off round the manège, at the walk. Each leading file in turn should trot and then canter as demonstrated, to join the rear of the ride. A few strides of canter are sufficient to begin with. Make a comment to each rider. Correct when necessary.
5. Change the rein, and repeat.
6. **Re-demonstrate**
7. **Play a game** – for example, 'Space Shuttles' (Fig. 15). The ride forms a large circle with the ponies' tails to the centre. Explain that the circle is in the earth and that each rider is on a launching pad which has room for one only. Then, for example, send 'Spacecraft Jane' to 'Spacecraft Richard's pad, orbiting left'. Jane then walks forward, turns left out of the circle, trots, and then canters round the outside of the circle. On approaching the opposite side of the circle to Richard, she trots and walks. As she goes across the circle and up

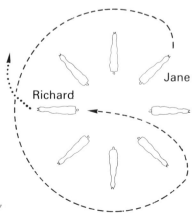

Fig. 15 'Space shuttles.'

behind Richard, he walks out, and might be told 'Spaceship Richard' to 'Spaceship Mary, orbit right'. Then 'Spaceship Mary' to '. . .', etc. Remind the ride that space shuttles are launched and docked slowly and with great precision (walking) and that they only go fast (canter) while in orbit. This game has many variations; other planets can be visited, etc.

7 Developing the Rider's Position

The correct position in the saddle is the essential basis for good riding. It is most important for the Instructor to read and understand fully 'The Position of the Rider in the Saddle' (*Manual of Horsemanship*).

The development of the correct position will take time. First the beginner should acquire feel and understanding for the pony, a living creature. Secondly he should begin to find his balance while riding. Balance cannot be taught, but the Instructor can help by encouraging each rider to find his own balanced position. At this stage, games and general fun are of more value than formal class lessons.

Without making the rider stiff or inhibited, the Instructor should demonstrate the correct position and should make corrections to basic faults such as crookedness.

The Instructor should foresee and avoid the risk of falls or frightening experiences, as they destroy the rider's natural suppleness and ease. Young riders who are growing fast are prone to set-backs; a balanced position during one holiday can become an unco-ordinated disaster the next. The Instructor must be sympathetic and must not allow the rider to become despondent. Awkward stages soon pass.

As balance and co-ordination improve, the rider will be able to feel almost a part of his horse. While retaining mobility of the hip joints and a supple back, his muscle control will develop so that he will be secure without excessive tension. Now he will be capable of applying the aids as he wishes, to direct or correct the horse. He will no longer give the wrong aids because he has lost his balance. The Instructor may then teach the correct contact of the rein and the more precise use of the leg and rein aids.

Once the rider is balanced, straight, supple and secure, he will have developed a good position.

TEACHING THE CORRECT POSITION is an important part of most lessons.

The following procedure might be useful during a lesson with a less experienced ride.

1. ***Explain*** why it is important to sit correctly, so that it is easy for the pony to carry the rider and to obey his aids. The aim of every rider should be to achieve a balanced, supple, and secure position. He will then be able to ride effectively and in harmony with his pony.

2. ***Demonstrate*** the correct position at the halt. It may help to show some common faults: the 'chair' seat and the 'fork' seat are obvious examples. (See Figs. 16, 17.) Explain why they make the rider less effective. Re-demonstrate the correct position.

3. ***Check*** each rider individually. Adjust stirrup leather lengths if necessary; check that they are of equal length, unless the rider has a physical defect which necessitates uneven leathers. Correct any basic faults. It is sometimes helpful to ask the rider to stand up in his stirrups after checking that the balls of his feet are on the stirrups. With supple knees and ankles, the rider will find his balance and what will generally be his correct leg position. If he then sits down gently into the saddle without moving his legs, he will be balanced, secure and comfortable.

4. ***Practise*** As soon as possible have the ride moving. Depending on the standard of the ride, practice might be in the form of a game, or a series of movements incorporating one or more paces.

5. ***Observe the riders*** from the side and from behind. Do not hurry your assessment, as riders sometimes take time to settle down. It helps to consider the following:
   a) Is each rider in control of his pony under the given circumstances?
   b) Is he in balance with his pony?
   c) Is he straight?
   d) Is he secure without undue tension?

6. ***Correct*** When noticing a fault in the rider's position, look for the root cause rather than the obvious effect. Most faults are caused by lack of balance: e.g., the rider with bouncing hands in rising trot will almost certainly be too tense through lack of balance. There would be no point in telling him to control his hands; he must first develop a balanced position. He will then be able to be more supple in his hips, back, and shoulders, which will lead to steadier hands. This will take time and practice. Anxiety and trying too hard will only inhibit progress. There is no immediate remedy, but physical exercises, particularly numbers 3 and 6, page 49 will help.

Riders should be asked to work on only one fault at a time. A long list of faults to be corrected is of little value. Often when the basic fault

is corrected the whole position will improve. Figs. 16, 17 and 19 show some common position faults. Figs. 18 and 20 show good positions.
TEACH THROUGH ENCOURAGEMENT RATHER THAN CRITICISM

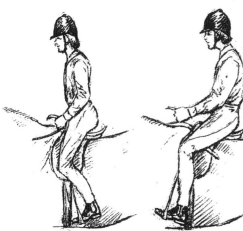

Fig. 16 'Fork' seat. Incorrect.

Fig. 17 'Chair' seat. Incorrect.

Fig. 18 Correct position.

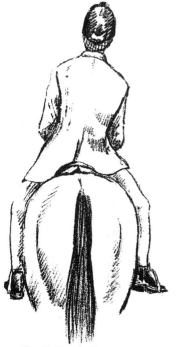

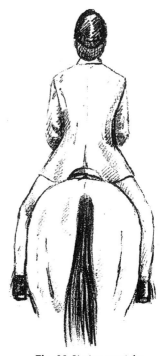

Fig. 19 Crooked seat. Incorrect.

Fig. 20 Sitting straight. Correct.

8   Physical Exercises

The object of physical exercises is to improve the rider's balance and security, thereby increasing his confidence. In most cases this is achieved by helping the rider to control the degree of relaxation and tension in individual muscles and joints, leading to a tension-free position of his body as a whole.

Physical exercises for a short period of the lesson are fun and useful to the ride provided that:

☐ The horses/ponies are settled and quiet enough to be safe.
☐ The ride is given frequent short intervals of rest, during and between each exercise. Use the period of relaxation between exercises to explain the next exercise.
☐ The exercises chosen are suitable for the age and standard of the ride.
☐ They come at an appropriate time in the lesson.

JUNIOR RIDES enjoy them during or towards the end of the lesson. Have plenty of help to lead the ponies, and to steady the riders.

Traditional favourites such as 'round the world', 'scissors', leaning forward on the pony's neck, lying back on his rump, kneeling on the saddle, etc., are performed at the halt. These are taught at most rallies and not described here.

MIDDLE AND SENIOR RIDES find exercises beneficial after the working-in period when the ponies are settled and will co-operate by moving slowly and rhythmically.

WORK WITHOUT STIRRUPS will be more comfortable if the stirrup leather buckles are pulled down about 4 inches (10 cms) from the stirrup bars before crossing the stirrups over the withers.

NOTE: Some ponies may be nervous when their riders stretch their arms high, or move in an unusual way. If you are unsure how the ponies will react, start with exercise 3(a) below before doing work without stirrups.

A FEW EXERCISES USED FOR SPECIFIC PURPOSES

1. *To ease tension in the neck*. Using stirrups and with both hands on the reins, the rider turns his head slowly from side to side. The rest of his body remains in the correct position.
2. *To stretch the arms, legs and back*. At the halt or walk, with one hand on the reins, and without stirrups, the rider slowly stretches his free arm up as high as he can, at the same time stretching his

legs down, with his toes as low as possible. He rests, changes his reins over, and repeats the exercise with the other arm.

3. ***To ease tension and to straighten the shoulders***. (a) Using stirrups and with the reins in one hand, the rider lets his free arm hang by his side. He then swings it rhythmically forwards, backwards, forwards, up and over. He repeats the exercise, rests, changes his reins over, and practises with the other arm.

   (b) Walking on a loose rein, the rider shrugs his shoulders and then rests. He repeats this several times.

   (c) *At the halt or walk, with stirrups and with reins knotted on the pony's neck, the rider sits up straight with his hands on his waist. He swings his left elbow and shoulder forward three times, allowing the right elbow and shoulder to go back, but keeping his head straight. He then swings his right elbow and shoulder forward and repeats the exercise several times.

4. ****To exercise the muscles in the waist ('aeroplanes')***. At the halt or walk, with stirrups, but with the reins knotted on the pony's neck, the rider stretches his arms out at shoulder height. He turns his upper body including his head, quite slowly from side to side.

5. ***To ease tension in the ankle-joints and to open the hips***. At the walk, on a long rein, without stirrups, the rider turns his toes up, in, down, and out, in a smooth circular movement of the ankles.

6. ***To ease tension in the lower part of the back and the hip-joints***.

   (a) Sitting trot without stirrups. At first the rider may hook one or two fingers under the front arch of the saddle to give him confidence and to get the feel of sitting in rhythm and in balance with the pony. He should concentrate on keeping his loins and hips supple to absorb the movement. His knees and ankles should be relaxed and he should keep his lower leg well down.

   As this exercise is strenuous, give the ride frequent periods of rest. Check each rider's position carefully, watching particularly for gripping upwards with the back of the calf which is wrong. Correct those who bump instead of sitting down in the centre of their saddles.

   (b) Without stirrups, in walk or sitting trot, the outside hand on the reins, the rider touches his inside toe with his inside hand without altering his feet position. It should be done on both reins.

7. ***To attain a deeper seat by opening the hips and riding with the thigh flat against the saddle***. This is carried out at the halt or walk, without stirrups. With his outside hand holding the reins, the fingers

---

*Important These two exercises should be carried out with discretion and only in an enclosed space.

49

of his inside hand under the saddle arch, the rider opens his legs (thighs and knees) slightly away from the saddle, draws them slightly back, and returns them to the saddle as they move forward, so that the large muscle under the thigh is pressed back behind the thigh, allowing it to lie flat on the saddle. Many riders, particularly those with round thighs, use this exercise while riding with or without stirrups, to correct their positions.

8. ***To ease tension in the knees***. At the walk on a long rein, without stirrups, the rider swings his lower legs (from the knee down) alternately forwards and backwards. His lower legs should be free from the pony's sides and he should maintain a low, still knee position on the saddle.

DURING ALL THE ABOVE EXERCISES CHECK THAT:

1. Each rider understands how to do the exercise properly. It may be helpful to discuss, demonstrate, and practise the exercises at the halt, before trying them at the walk or trot.
2. Except for the part of him involved in the exercise, the rider does not compromise his correct basic position: e.g., when swinging one arm, the rest of his body should remain square with his weight carried equally on both seat bones. His seat and legs should be in the correct position and he should take care not to make any inadvertent movements.
3. The rider does not use his reins as a life-line, even in an emergency. Should he lose his balance, he may hold on by the saddle-arch, the mane or a neckstrap, but never by the reins.

Exercises become more difficult if practised without stirrups or at a faster pace, e.g. trot instead of walk. Use them according to the standard of the ride. Additional exercises for work on the lunge are on page 127.

Jumping

9 Instruction in Jumping

THE INSTRUCTOR'S AIMS

1. ENSURE SAFETY. Double check tack. See that hats fit correctly. Knot reins which are too long. Neckstraps (for details on fitting, see page 39) should be used for beginners who might otherwise pull the pony in the mouth during the unaccustomed feel of the take-off. Ensure that poles are smooth and that metal fittings are removed from stands unless poles are resting on them. It is safest to give the jumping lesson in an enclosed area. Remember to shut the gate. Use your common sense to ward off a potentially dangerous situation before an accident happens.

2. INSTIL CONFIDENCE. Confidence is laboriously built but easily destroyed. It is important to avoid falls. Ponies jump best over fences which look solid, imposing and inviting. Ground lines are helpful. Plan the lesson so that steady progress is made, with the most challenging fences or problems tackled three-quarters of the way through the lesson. There will then be time to correct mistakes and restore confidence if necessary.

3. MAKE IMPROVEMENT. Riding over fences is usually improved by correcting basic riding faults, and by improving the quality of work on the flat. It is unnecessary and a waste of time to find out how high each pony can jump. The ride should not be over-faced, but enough interesting problems should be solved to leave the riders with a sense of achievement.

THE POSITION OF THE RIDE AND THE INSTRUCTOR

Jumping lessons consist of work on the flat and jumping. The position of the Instructor and the ride during work on the flat is covered on page 28.

When the ride is jumping, with few exceptions, each member will perform individually.

It is important, especially when taking a less experienced ride, for the Instructor to keep an eye on the ride as well as to watch the member who is practising.

The following diagrams show situations where single fences are in use, but the same principles apply when the Instructor is using further fences, trotting poles, or gymnastic jumps.

The riders should be told the shape of the whole exercise, where to go and at what pace, from the time their turn starts until they rejoin the ride.

When taking advanced rides, the Instructor may sometimes suggest independent work for the riders between turns.

With less advanced riders, those who are waiting for their turns should stand still in a ride, and may be asked for comment, thus learning by watching.

Island Fences

The ride is positioned where it can watch, and the Instructor stands on the opposite side of the fence.

Fig. 21 shows the positioning of the ride and the Instructor, and the shape of a basic exercise, with the correct line of approach coming off a half-circle to the centre of the fence.

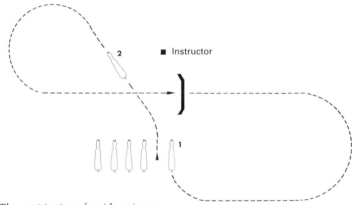

Fig. 21 The positioning of a ride using an island fence.

Fence alongside a Hedge

Sometimes the fence is flush against a hedge or the wall of an indoor school. This is an advantage for junior riders as it helps them to keep their ponies straight. Check that the ponies cannot run out between the hedge and the fence, and build a wing on the open side of the fence. The Instructor must still be in a position to watch the performing member and the rest of the ride. This may mean changing the normal sitings of the ride.

Pairs of markers are helpful in keeping the very young on the correct lines before and after the fence. Cones are ideal, but heavy upturned plastic buckets with handles removed are a good substitute.

Fig. 22 illustrates the positioning of the ride and the Instructor when the fence is against a hedge or wall. The exercise shown is suitable for junior riders, with the markers ensuring a correct line.

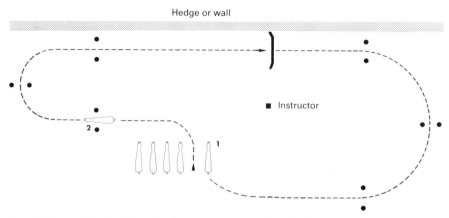

Fig. 22 The positioning of a ride using a fence alongside a hedge.

With a Junior Ride of more than 8 Members

If the ride is large, there will be a considerable lapse of time between a pony's first jump and his next. During this period he may get cold and stiff, and the result may well be an unnecessary stop. The following technique overcomes the problem and enables two ponies to be working at the same time.

Fig 23a. Riders 1 and 2 are sent out to ride at the trot in a circle.

Fig 23b. On command, rider 1 peels off the circle, jumps the fence, goes straight forward 8 to 10 yards (7 to 9 metres), and halts. There is always a danger that on landing a pony will turn sharply to hurry back to the ride. The Instructor must insist that the pony is ridden straight forward so that the rider will learn to be in control on the landing side of the fence. The danger of a slip-up and fall will thus be avoided. The pony's presence on the far side of a fence acts as a 'carrot' to Rider 2's pony. Rider 3 moves out to trot round behind Rider 2.

Fig 23c. Rider 2, in his turn, lands over the fence and replaces Rider 1, who moves off to take up his original place in the ride.
Rider 4 will have moved out behind Rider 3. Continue this until all have jumped.

The Instructor can make his comments to riders either when they have halted or when they return to the ride.

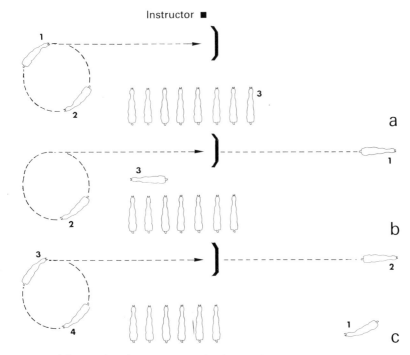

Fig. 23 A useful way of working a junior ride of more than eight members.

With a large, more competent ride

Follow the same procedure as above, but, according to circumstances, keep the whole ride on the move in a large circle at walk or trot when not jumping.

ALWAYS MAKE A COMMENT TO EACH RIDER AFTER HIS TURN EVEN IF ONLY TO SAY 'WELL DONE'.

PLANNING THE JUMPING LESSON

1. Your 'aims' – to ensure safety, instil confidence, and bring about improvement – should be kept firmly in mind.
2. Explain why jumping lessons do not entirely consist of jumping.
3. Use the structure as described in 'Procedure' on page 34.
4. Plan to include circles and other movements designed to make the ponies balanced, supple and obedient at the beginning of and during the lesson.
5. Remember that it is important to keep working on the riders' positions. (See 'The Rider's Position when Jumping', page 59).
6. When instructing large numbers use shorter exercises so that there is less time for each rider to wait between his turns.

The quality of jumping for the pony depends on the quality of flat work between fences.

The quality of jumping for the rider depends on his ability to produce good work on the flat between the fences and to stay secure, balanced and in harmony with his pony at all times including the approach, jump and recovery. Video used correctly is helpful. (See pages 80–82.)

TAKING A JUMPING LESSON

If the ride has reached the stage when stirrup leathers are to be shortened for jumping, this should be done at the beginning of the lesson.

Assessing the ride by its work on the flat can be misleading. Many ponies and riders will change their attitudes and their balance at the sight of a fence.

a) **With juniors** Walk the ride, about six ponies' lengths from each other, on a loose rein over a single pole on the ground. The ponies who break into a trot, or in other ways play up, when they see the pole will probably rush when faced with a fence. Those who trip over the pole may well prove to be sluggish.

b) **With average and senior rides** After working in the ride, introduce a small but solid-looking fence. Do not use a wall or a fence with a fixed base until you know the capabilities of the ride. At first they should jump from the trot. One or two canter strides before and after the fence are permissible. The way the ride performs this simple exercise will indicate how the ponies and riders react to jumping.

With all but the beginners' rides, treat schooling fences as part of a movement on the flat so that they are negotiated with the minimum amount of fuss.

- Work on perfecting the whole movement, not merely the jump.
- Two fences incorporated into a movement help the ride to establish a rhythmical canter between fences.
- Aim to teach a smooth, balanced rhythmical approach, impulsive enough to jump the height required. The pony will then make his own arrangements to arrive at the correct spot for take-off. Although the development of an 'eye for a stride' is desirable especially in show jumping, when accuracy is at a premium – erratic attempts to 'find a stride' will usually end in disaster, until the rider can adjust the length of stride without upsetting the pony's rhythm and balance.
- Check that each member can produce a pace of sufficient impulsion to jump the fence. More impulsion is needed when the fence is on an uphill gradient. Heavy ponies need more impulsion than light ones.

- Know when to stop. Finish jumping BEFORE ponies and riders get tired and their work deteriorates.
- Reserve some time for ensuring the success of the last exercise and for cooling off the ponies. The lesson should finish on a happy note.
- See that the ponies are rewarded for good work. A word spoken kindly or a pat on the neck helps to settle a nervous pony, boosts confidence, and confirms in the pony's mind that he has done well, provided that the reward is given immediately after the good work.
- Members of more advanced rides should dismount immediately after halting from the final, successful, exercise, as this equates in the ponies' minds the reward – which is the relief from carrying weight – with the correct way of going.
- Whenever it is practical, all rides should dismount and lead in.
- If the last exercise is strenuous or involves galloping, more cooling off time will be needed.

TEACHING RIDERS TO JUMP

1. Read 'Instructing Beginners and the Very Young', page 39.
2. Neckstraps should be used. (For fitting see page 39.)
3. As the pony jumps, and on landing, the rider should have little contact through the reins until the position is established sufficiently for the contact to be consistent and sympathetic.
4. In the meantime, teach the riders what to do when their ponies jump. Demonstrate at the halt how the riders should:
   - ☐ Look straight ahead.
   - ☐ Hold the neckstrap.
   - ☐ Swing forward from the hips.
5. After practising this at the halt, try it at the walk over two poles on the ground about 6 metres (20ft) apart, preferably alongside a hedge or fence. Put out markers in pairs to show the correct lines of approach. (See Figure 22.)
6. It is useful to have helpers at the beginning and end of the approach, especially if some members of the ride are just off the leading-rein.
7. Demonstrate, or send an assistant to demonstrate, the 'course' through the markers and over the poles. Show how each rider will perform the three actions described above, as the ponies walk over the poles. The ride may then practise individually.
8. Ask the ride to point out if the member who is performing fails to carry out any of the three actions. This will hold their attention and teach them to learn by observing what others do.
9. The ride may be advanced enough to trot or to canter over a small

obstacle, with a ground-line, alongside the fence or hedge. The ponies will make a hop or a small jump.

10. At this stage retain the markers and the helpers, because the riders must concentrate on keeping in harmony with their ponies as they jump.

11. End the pre-jumping lesson with a game, such as 'Pass the Password', in which the poles must be negotiated, as part of a course set out with the markers, before the password can be given to the next 'messenger'.

12. Those who are able to jump small fences may finish with a game such as 'Relay'. Each rider trots away from the ride, turns round a helper, and trots back over a low fence. The next one starts immediately, as if practising for a relay race.

13. Ensure that the riders learn to reward their ponies by patting them, either soon after landing, or – if that would be unsafe – on returning to the ride.

NOTE: With just three actions to carry out, the beginner will, from the start, assume a correct position, and should never have such problems as making strange contortions or fixing the hands as the pony jumps, remembering:

☐ Look forward.
☐ Hands forward.
☐ Swing forward.

ENCOURAGING PONIES TO JUMP WELL

Riders and ponies influence each other. If the pony is performing calmly and fluently, it is easier to teach the rider. Use the following points to encourage every pony to jump well.

a) Ponies jump more correctly in a flat area over a solid-looking fence with a ground-line on the take-off side. Fences should therefore be built with substantial top rails, ground-lines, and a diagonal pole or cross-poles between the two (Fig. 24).

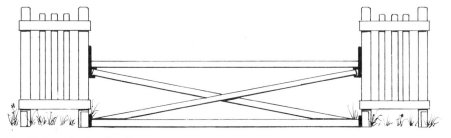

Fig. 24 A good schooling fence.

b) Less substantial fences are needed for small ponies, which may otherwise tend to jump too high for their small riders.
c) Less experienced rides may need a 'carrot' on the landing side of the fence.
d) It sometimes helps to give a pony a lead, but choose a reliable one.
e) The best approach is usually from a large half-circle on to a straight line, to the centre of the fence. The length of the straight line may be varied. Impetuous ponies jump best off a short approach.

Having identified the lazy and the impetuous, treat them accordingly. Encourage the riders in particular to concentrate on improving their riding rather than worrying about their ponies' problems. As they improve themselves, they will automatically improve their ponies, and be able to do more demanding work.

10   The Rider's Position When Jumping

See *The Manual of Horsemanship*: 'Analysis of the Jump', and 'The Rider's Position for Jumping'.

The rider's basic position does not change for jumping. After each rider's position has been assessed, the stirrup leathers should be shortened if necessary. This will close the angles at the hips, knees and ankles, which increases the security of the riders and helps them to stay in balance as their ponies jump.

DEVELOPING THE RIDER'S POSITION WHEN JUMPING

The correct position is developed over a period of months or even years, first by acquiring a secure but tension-free position when riding on the flat. This enables the rider to control the approach, in both the quality of the pace and the accuracy of the chosen track or path to the fence and after it.

With practice, the rider becomes familiar with the feel of jumping, by:
(a) Swinging forward from the hips to reciprocate the thrust of the take-off.
(b) Allowing with the hands (also elbows and shoulders if necessary) as the pony's head and neck stretch forward.

(c) Absorbing most of the shock through knees and ankles as the pony lands.

(d) Remaining in balance, while the recovery stride leads to the re-establishment of the pace used in the approach.

The beginner must firstly develop confidence and balance by riding to, over, and away from very small fences.

At first the neckstrap can be held *before* the take-off. Later it can be held *during* the take-off. Eventually the rider will be secure enough to jump without the neckstrap, keeping a light contact with the reins. By now the rider's legs will be more effective and he will be able to learn how to improve his pony's paces.

He can now be taught how to make a correct, impulsive approach, which will improve the quality of the pony's jump. Ideally this is the path along which progress should be made, but only too often the Instructor will be confronted by riders and ponies whose problems require long term re-training.

Listed below are some of the more common problems with suggestions for immediate action by the Instructor:

COMMON FAULTS

In the Approach

1. *Rider allowing pony to rush his fences*
FAULT (a) The rider is left behind the movement, his loss of balance and his tension causing involuntary driving aids.
CORRECTION Teach the rider, perhaps with the use of the neckstrap, to sit quietly and to go with the pony. Make him aware that he should not give any accidental or unnecessary driving aids.
FAULT (b) The rider habitually shortens his reins just before starting the approach. This becomes a signal to the pony who accelerates while the rider is still sorting out his reins.
CORRECTION The rider should, if necessary, adjust his reins in good time before turning on to the approach.

2. *Impetuous pony rushing his fences regardless of the rider's aids*
FAULT Poor training, or fear.
CORRECTION (a) The rider should trot the pony in a circle in front of the fence.
(b) He should stroke the pony with his outside hand, the outside of his fingers moving up and down the pony's neck, without changing the position of his hand on the

rein, or his weight in the saddle. This will help to relieve tension.

(c) He should continue circling until the pony is trotting quietly and rhythmically, gradually edging the circle closer to the fence.

(d) He should come quietly off the circle without changing his balance, and should then jump the fence.

(e) This should be repeated at several other fences which are well within the pony's capabilities. Impetuous ponies jump best from short approaches and going away from home or from the gate.

3. *The pony decelerating and losing impulsion just before take-off*

FAULT (a) The pony – who may be lacking in confidence or lazy – shifts the insecure rider forward into a position where he is unable to correct him. The pony may then refuse, run out, or jump badly.

CORRECTION Teach the rider to maintain the pace of the approach, particularly in the last few strides, when he may have to drive the pony forward firmly with his legs. If necessary the leg aid may be reinforced by the whip, used behind the leg.

FAULT (b) The rider approaching from too far away.

CORRECTION Let him walks his pony towards the fence from about 14 metres, breaking into a trot and finally into canter for 3 or 4 strides. This helps the rider to control the approach and to keep the pony's hocks engaged.

4. *The rider looking down and concentrating on the bottom of a fence or ditch*. (This often causes refusals or poor jumping).

FAULT Apprehension or bad habit.

CORRECTION Ask a dismounted assistant to stand on the landing side of the fence and to hold up his hand as the rider approaches the fence. Tell the rider to ride forward with determination, to look up, and to call out how many fingers the assistant is showing.

5. *The rider unbalancing the pony during the approach*

Any sudden or untactful alterations in the rider's balance or contact during a good approach will cause the pony to lose concentration, and will upset his rhythm and balance, thereby spoiling the jump.

FAULT (a) Insecure position.

CORRECTION Guidance in improving the position and practising the approach will eventually help the situation. Immediate improvement can be made by use of the neckstrap.

FAULT (b) Rider swinging forward, the reins becoming loose in anticipation of the take-off. This causes the pony to become unbalanced on to his forehand, from where it is difficult for him to jump.

CORRECTION Use the neckstrap to give the rider more confidence so that he will not make any alterations in his balance or contact just before the take-off.

FAULT (c) Rider habitually interfering with the pony's stride and rhythm during the approach.

CORRECTION Take the fence away, and let the rider practise maintaining a correct pace between the wings of the fence. Then, as he continues cantering on the circle, build the fence. The rider will then find out how much easier it is for his pony to jump when concentration is not interrupted.

FAULT (d) Continuous steady pulling on the reins by the rider during the approach, usually caused by anticipation, and which develops into a habit. The pony, feeling the continuous drag on his mouth, often pulls back. Leaning hard on the rider's hands, he then drops his weight on to the forehand, which makes taking off difficult.

CORRECTION Let the rider practise jumping over a combination, either in a jumping lane or alongside a hedge or wall, without holding the reins. (When jumping without reins the ride should be in an enclosed area.) This improves the rider's balance and confidence. He soon learns that he and his pony perform better when they are not having a tug-of-war. Alternatively a neckstrap should be used.

6. *The pony running out*

The rider loses control in the approach and is unable to hold the pony straight when he dives quickly to one side of the fence.

FAULT The rider's legs and hands are not effective enough to hold the determined pony straight (Fig. 25a).

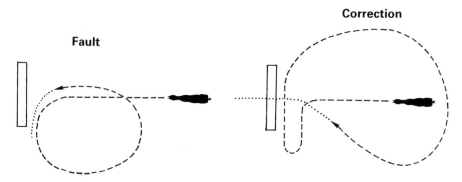

Fig. 25a The wrong track to take when a pony runs out to the left.

Fig. 25b The right track to take when a pony runs out to the left.

CORRECTION (a)   The rider should turn the pony in the opposite direction to that in which he ran out.

    (b)   Make sure that the whip is carried at the side on which the pony ran out.

    (c)   The pony should be walked towards the centre of the fence at an angle of 45 degrees from the side on which he ran out, breaking into trot and finally into canter.

    (d)   The pony will swing in the same direction as before, will find himself square with the fence, and will jump it. (Fig. 25b).

    (e)   If the approach is kept at a slow pace the pony will be less likely to get out of control.

The final cure is obviously for the rider to improve the effectiveness of his legs and hands in holding the pony straight.

During the Jump

1. *The rider loses balance in front of or behind the movement*

FAULT (a) *In front of the movement.* The rider leans forward abruptly, anticipating the take-off. This unbalances the pony on to his forehand and causes him to take an extra re-balancing stride before taking off. The rider is then unbalanced during the jump.

FAULT (b) *Getting left behind.* The rider expects the pony to take another stride, and sometimes sits stiffly upright with tight reins, trying to shorten the strides. The pony reacts to this inadvertently given driving aid through the rider's seat, and takes off a stride early. The rider gets left behind and unless he *slips the reins*, jabs the pony in the mouth.

CORRECTIONS (a) and (b). Use a series of small fences alongside a hedge or wall. With less need to control the pony, the rider will be able to concentrate on feeling the movement of the pony and improving his position. He will also learn to feel the difference in the movement of the take-off stride. If he is in balance and secure at all times, he will be able to retain his position wherever the pony takes off.

Slipping the reins

More competent riders should be shown how to slip the reins and collect them again. In an emergency, when more rein is needed by the pony than the rider is able to give at that moment, the rider should open his fingers and allow the reins to slip through. He should collect them up again as soon as possible after landing by taking the buckle with one hand and pulling the reins back through the fingers of the other hand, which should remain in the correct position.

63

This can be practised:

(a) at the halt and then at the walk, making the change between loose rein walk and medium walk.

(b) with the rider sitting on a chair, his eyes closed, holding the reins as if riding. The Instructor takes the bit-ends of the reins and moves them from or towards the rider, whose hands must follow. When the reins are suddenly pulled away – as they would be if the rider were to be left behind or if the pony stumbled on landing – the rider must slip the reins.

2. *The rider fixes his hands or pulls on the reins*

If the rider's hands do not follow the movement of the pony's head and neck, either during take-off or throughout the whole of the jump, the pony will be forced to flatten or hollow his back.

FAULT (a) Rider holding on by the reins because he has not yet developed a secure position.

CORRECTION A neckstrap should be used.

FAULT (b) Rider has developed a bad habit – such as keeping his hands locked into his stomach or pulling the pony in the mouth during the take-off.

CORRECTION Use jumping lanes or small fences alongside a hedge or wall, the rider practising without holding the reins and with his arms crossed.

OR

Sit the rider on a chair, as suggested above for 'Slipping the Reins' but use smooth movements so that the rider learns to follow the movement of the pony's head and neck with his hands.

3. *The rider adopts incorrect leg positions*

If the rider stands up in the stirrups or tips on to his knees with his lower legs swinging back and up, the pony will be unbalanced during the jump.

FAULT Rider not folding forward from the hips. This is due to:

• Apprehension, which causes tension.
• The mistaken idea that radical movements will make the pony jump higher.

CORRECTION The rider should practise swinging forward from the hips while riding on the flat. He should then practise jumping doubles or gymnastic jumps, which do not allow time for incorrect movements.

4. *The rider fails to keep his body straight*

FAULT The rider swings his weight to one side and looks down the pony's shoulder, which unbalances the pony.

CORRECTION First check that the rider is sitting square and straight while riding on the flat. Provide something on the landing side which the rider must watch as he jumps, so that he will look forward and straight between his pony's ears. (See correction 4 on page 61).

On Landing

1. *The rider's body collapses forward*
FAULT The rider does not absorb through his knees and ankles the change in the direction of the movement.
CORRECTION Physical exercises on the flat, to reduce tension in the joints, will help. The rider should practise standing up in his stirrups with knees and ankles relaxed and as low as possible. Tell him to try to feel this relaxation as the pony lands. Then, if possible, work through a combination of small fences to practise the feel of absorbing the shock of landing over consecutive obstacles.

2. *The rider rounds his back and flops on to the pony's loins*
The pony lands, stops as the rider flops on to the back of the saddle, and has difficulty in re-balancing and moving forward.
FAULT (a) The stirrup leathers are too long. (b) The rider is tired, or so surprised and thankful at having reached the landing side of the fence that he loses his concentration.
CORRECTION Check the length of the stirrup leathers. Then let the rider trot up to the fence, jump it, and canter away from it. Alternatively, use a double, which will make the rider stay in balance to jump the second element correctly.

COMMON PROBLEMS

Lack of Confidence
The building of confidence should always be in the forefront of the Instructor's mind. Confidence may be lost by:
(a) A fall. Riders who have a fall as a result of carrying out the Instructor's orders will quickly lose confidence in themselves and in the Instructor.
(b) A bad jump which caused pain to the pony and/or the rider.
(c) Natural timidity.
The situation sometimes becomes worse as pony and rider convince each other of their lack of ability to jump even the smallest obstacle.
CORRECTION (a) Make the fences very easy.
(b) Use a reliable member of the ride to give a lead.
(c) The rider who has problems should hold the neckstrap.

(d) With more experienced riders, the exercise 'Gymnastics without trotting-poles', page 124, might be helpful.

HAZARDS TO AVOID

Do not allow the ride to lose confidence through the following:

☐ Overfacing. If a fence proves to be too difficult for a pony or rider at their particular stage of training it must be reduced in its dimensions, and confidence must be regained by jumping the smaller fence.

☐ Slippery going. Rain after a long period of dry weather causes slippery going, which may unbalance ponies and affect their confidence. Choose approach and landing areas with care, and reduce the size of fences.

☐ Wrong distances. When using a double make sure that the distance is satisfactory for the ponies in the ride before making the fences more difficult or before adding a third.

Pain No pony will jump correctly if he is in pain. Be particularly aware of any signs of lameness, sore backs, or sore mouths. Pain may be the cause of reluctance to move forward or anxiety to complete the jump as quickly as possible. Note that though pain causes tension, tense ponies are not always in pain.

If a pony which normally performs well starts to refuse, he should be examined carefully for any illness or injury which may be causing pain. Ponies which are obviously in pain should not be allowed to jump. Help should be given if possible. Otherwise, veterinary advice should be sought.

11 Jumping Exercises Needing a Small Amount of Equipment

At rallies, the ideal amount of fence-building material is seldom available to every ride. The following exercises show some ways in which useful jumping lessons can be given, even to advanced rides, using the minimum amount of equipment. When poles and stands are scarce, it is usually better to build one substantial fence than two flimsy ones.

1. Jumping from Trot

• This is an essential part of the jumping lesson.

- It may be performed with or without the help of trotting-poles.
- Senior rides will benefit from the use of trotting-poles as long as the horses in the ride have strides of a similar length, and equipment is available to make at least four trotting-poles and one fence. See 'Trotting-poles and Gymnastic Jumping', page 118.
- Alternatively, teach the ride to approach a single fence in a steady, rhythmical, rising trot.
- One or two strides of canter before and after the fence may be permitted.
- Jumping from the trot is important because:
  (a) It is a useful limbering-up exercise, allowing the ponies to stretch their muscles without becoming excited.
  (b) It teaches the ponies to jump off their hocks.
  (c) A balanced approach in trot is the forerunner of a balanced approach in canter. It is therefore a stage in teaching a young or unbalanced pony to jump correctly
  (d) It gives riders and ponies confidence to know that they can jump competently at a slow pace. This is particularly important on a cross-country course, where some fences may have to be tackled slowly.
  (e) Jumping from trot then cantering on landing is a useful exercise, especially for those who ride up to a fence but stop riding forward at the last moment, causing their ponies to stop or just struggle over.

2. Jumping off a Circle If the ride is capable of achieving a reasonable 30-metre circle in canter, a useful exercise may be performed by including a fence on the circle.

(a) In turn, each rider canters a circle, leaving the fence on the outside, until the impulsion, rhythm, and balance are correct.

(b) Without losing the bend, he enlarges the circle slightly to include the fence, continuing afterwards on the circle without changing the pace. Most members will make three circles, jumping the fence on the second circuit. If a pony rushes at the fence, or otherwise breaks the rhythm of the canter, the rider should turn inside the fence until the rhythm is re-established.

(c) The exercise should be carried out on both reins. If space is limited, use the same circle and a fence which is jumpable from both directions, such as a 'hog's back'.

If the riders are advanced enough to work independently, several members may perform at once, each with his own fence. However, each rider will jump only when commanded by the Instructor, who will then watch that particular individual. The others will continue to canter in circles until they, in turn, are told to jump. The circles should not overlap. Beware of keeping any pony cantering for too long.

3. Doubles. Simple doubles at correct distances promote rhythm and balance. They teach the rider to:

(a) Maintain his position.

(b) Ride forward.

(c) Ride straight to the centre of the second element.

Equipment required A minimum of two pairs of stands and four poles.

- After some preliminary movements and jumping the ride over a single fence, build a double with 10 metres (approx. 33 ft) between the two fences. Keep the fences small until you are sure that the distance is satisfactory.

- It is most unlikely that the ponies in a ride will have strides of identical length. It will, therefore, be impossible to build a double which is perfect for the whole ride.

- If the average height is 14hh, the free-moving ponies will take two non-jumping strides, and those with shorter strides will have room to make three, without breaking their rhythm.

- If the double is on a gradient, the distance will need to be slightly shorter when approached uphill, and longer when going downhill.

- Use the fence from both directions, but remember to change the ground-lines.

- A one non-jumping stride double may be built if the ponies have similar lengths of stride.

- Start with the fence at 6.25 metres (approx. 20½ ft) apart but be prepared to adjust the distance so that the ponies jump it easily in their stride. Those with more ability may need 7.25 metres (almost 24 ft).

4. Cross Poles These encourage the ride to make a habit of jumping in the centre of their fences. Fences may be made more challenging by adjusting the angle and the height in the centre.

They are useful as a training aid and fun for all rides to jump.

Having jumped them successfully from a normal approach, more advanced rides may jump the fences as the centre of a figure-of-eight, in trot or canter.

- The ride should first achieve acceptable circles in trot and canter on both reins.

- Each rider in turn may then practise a figure-of-eight, first in trot and then in canter, without the poles in place, changing the leg through trot between the jump stands.

- Then try it with the cross poles in place.

- The ponies will generally land with the other leg leading.

- Unless the ponies have been well schooled, these exercises will prove difficult.

- Two or three lessons may be needed because an acceptable standard must be reached at each stage before progressing to the next.
- The exercise is valuable because it teaches the riders to:
  (a) Ride circles.
  (b) Straighten their ponies.
  (c) Develop the opposite bend.

5. Counting Strides Middle rides enjoy an exercise which includes counting 'Three, two, one, jump' during the last few strides of the approach, which in this case should be straight and in canter. The exercise is helpful in teaching judgment of distances and lengths of stride. By calling 'jump' on the take-off stride, the rider will learn the difference in feel between it and the non-jumping strides. Counting strides also helps to maintain a constant rhythm and prevents the rider from holding his breath.

Procedure

- Ensure that the ride is performing fluently over the fence.
- Tell the riders to call 'jump' during the take-off stride.
- Make them count the last few strides.
- The riders should not interfere with their ponies in order to make their counting correct.

6. Gradients If there is a hollow or a hill in the field, the ride may be taught how to compensate for the gradient, when jumping uphill and down. The fence should be low and fixed securely. A pole rolling downhill can cause an accident. Logs firmly wedged on both sides with small stakes are ideal. A wedged pole on the ground is a useful starter. Jump the ride uphill first. Some ponies may buck or run away downhill, until they have expended some energy.

- GOING UPHILL more impulsion will be needed. The ponies should, and generally will, take off nearer than usual to the fence, because the higher up the hill they get before taking off, the lower the fence will be. They should not be allowed to sprawl up the hill with their hocks out behind, as their hocks must be well engaged when they arrive at the place where they will take off.
- GOING DOWNHILL balance should be maintained and speed should be controlled. Less advanced rides should start downhill very slowly, to discourage their ponies from taking huge leaps and landing at the bottom. More advanced rides will do this by controlling the pace and keeping the length of stride short.

7. Ditches These are not ideal obstacles for beginners, but they sometimes need to be negotiated in the course of cross-country rides or while moving from one area to another at camp.

- Ponies sometimes jump big over ditches, so inexperienced riders should hold on to neckstraps.
- As no poles are involved, the ride may follow on at the walk with 3 or 4 lengths between each pony.
- A bold pony should be leading file.
- The riders should look forward into the next field. They should never look down into the bottom of the ditch.
- It helps if the ditch is first jumped towards home.
- Ponies are less apprehensive of natural, as opposed to artificial, ditches.
- It is not advisable for the Instructor to lead the pony over, as ponies sometimes jump into those leading them.
- It may be possible to lead the pony down an easier place into the ditch, along it, and up the other side.
- If a pony persistently refuses, the advice of a senior Instructor should be sought.

8. Jumping from Different Angles over Different Parts of the Fence
Young horses and less experienced riders should be taught to jump in the centre of their fences, but as training progresses, rides should be taught to vary the line of approach. Use one fence, two pieces of ribbon, and four markers. Cones are ideal, but logs, or plastic buckets with their handles removed, are an acceptable substitute. Tie the ribbons round the top pole of the fence one-third and two-thirds along.

(a) After some preliminary exercises, during which the fence is jumped straight and the ride is assessed, ask each rider to describe a correct arc and to jump the fence between the ribbon and the upright (Fig. 26) Line A. As always, insist that the ride works towards producing a smooth, balanced, rhythmical movement.

(b) If the ride proves that it can jump anywhere along the pole, and accurately over a ribbon, on a straight line, tell the riders to try jumping off a large circle, about 30 metres in diameter, inside the buckets and over the fence (Line B).

(c) Practise jumping the fence, between the ribbons, at an angle on a straight line from the inside of one marker to the inside of the diagonal marker (Line C). Note that though this line may appear to be straight when approaching to jump from left to right, the rider will have the pony bent slightly to the left. After the fence the pony will be bent to the right. Note that in Fig. 26 no arrows are shown, as each exercise may be performed either way. Remember to change the ground-lines.

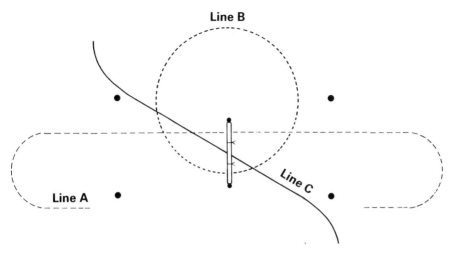

Fig. 26 Jumping from different angles over different parts of the fence.

These exercises can vary from simple to complicated, depending on the standard of the ride.

☐ Junior rides may perform them at a walk, with ribbons on the pole on the ground.

☐ Middle rides enjoy team games, with top marks scored by those who can describe a correct arc and jump a low fence over a ribbon.

SHOULD PROBLEMS ARISE, ALWAYS REVERT TO A STRAIGHT APPROACH TO THE CENTRE OF THE FENCE.

9. Jumping from Slow and Fast Speeds

Advanced rides may need to practise jumping at different speeds off different lengths of stride. The two extremes may be practised, using in each case a single fence. Suitable exercises are:

(A) *Jumping off a short stride in canter*

Use an upright fence which looks solid but will knock down. The strides should be full of impulsion and the rhythm active, although the speed is slow and the strides are short. This should be maintained through the whole movement.

- Reduce the length of approach to a minimum. The object is to teach the rider how to cope with short approaches, such as jumping out of country lanes when hunting. Also, ponies often become frustrated cantering slowly on a long approach.
- Put a marker a few strides from the fence.
- Each rider should approach the marker at the correct pace, at a right-

angle to the fence. Then he should turn inside the marker and jump the fence.

- A correct bend is essential.
- The exercise should be carried out on both reins.
- After the ride has completed the exercise successfully, quick turns may be practised on the landing side to simulate jumping into a lane.
- Following this demanding exercise, work the ride over a larger staircase fence, off a normal stride, to re-establish free forward movement.

(B) *Jumping from the gallop*

This should be taught only by senior Instructors who will first ensure that exercises using a normal schooling fence have been completed satisfactorily, and that a well-built steeplechase fence – which leans away from the take-off – is available.

Teach the ride to gallop at a balanced, rhythmical pace, using the correct galloping position, before attempting to jump. Horses will find their own strides at the gallop as long as they are allowed to concentrate during the approach. Riders should therefore sit still, keeping an even contact but ready to react immediately to any variation in the pace.

Jumping from the gallop should be the last exercise of the lesson.

Leave time for the horses to cool off.

Taking The
Dismounted Ride

12 Instruction in Horsemastership

The ride must understand that horsemastership in all its aspects is of vital importance. Without good horsemastership, no pony, however talented, and well ridden will ever achieve its full potential. Ignorance can lead to suffering and can cause lasting damage. Because horsemastership does not come naturally and requires mental effort and application, it must be taught in an interesting way.

The Dismounted Group Lesson
By far the most satisfactory way of teaching horsemastership is by giving practical lessons, using either members' own ponies and equipment or, if it is a dismounted rally, some pre-planned facilities.
Preparation
Find out the following:
(a) THE RIDE The ages, standards, and number of riders in the group.
(b) FACILITIES Where the lesson will be held. What props will be available, and what items you need to supply.
(c) TIME How long the lesson will be.
(d) SUBJECT The Chief Instructor will tell you the subject (e.g. clipping or feeding) that is to be taught. Otherwise, make your own decision according to (a), (b), and (c) above.

READ the relevant parts of the current *Manual of Horsemanship* and take notes of the main points.
CHOOSE those aspects which apply to the standard and age of the ride.
PLAN how you will give an entertaining talk and demonstration. These should, as a rule, take one-quarter of the lesson time, leaving three-quarters in which the ride can practise.

Instructors should insist on high standards of practical work from the ride, as this will increase interest and pride in the results.

NOTE: Be aware of weather conditions. The ride will not pay attention if they are too cold or too wet or too hot.

GROOMING

This sample lesson is suitable for any riders aged 6 to 12 who keep their ponies stabled or at grass.

74

The lesson will take place at a day rally or on the first day of camp after a mounted lesson. Each member should have a headcollar with rope, and a complete grooming kit. If the ponies are to be turned out at night, avoid grooming their backs too thoroughly as this removes the protective natural grease.

Before the Lesson
Choose a safe place for the ponies to be tied up, e.g. along a fence in a field, or in an enclosed yard. Decide (a) which pony and grooming kit you will borrow for your demonstration, (b) where you will tie the pony, (c) where you will lay out the grooming kit and (d) where the class will sit, so that everyone can watch and hear you easily.

Taking the Lesson
After seeing that the ponies are unsaddled and tied up correctly, lay out the grooming kit on a table or straw bale and begin your lesson.
You should deal with:
1. THE REASONS FOR GROOMING Involve the group by asking questions.
2. HOW TO PREPARE FOR GROOMING Check how the pony to be used for the demonstration is tied up. Take off hats and coats and put them in a clean, safe place. If it is warm, roll up sleeves.
3. THE NAMES AND USES OF EACH ITEM OF GROOMING KIT Ask the group to tell you the names of the items. Demonstrate the correct use of each item by grooming one side of the pony, but be sure to point out that in reality both sides should be groomed!
4. PRACTICE Each member should groom his own pony while you watch and correct faults. The pony which you have used for demonstrating will have the other side groomed by his rider. Remember that very young members will need help.
5. At the end of the period take a few minutes (a) to *ask* a few questions, to satisfy yourself that the main points have been absorbed, and (b) to *answer* any questions.

The above has been explained in detail to show how this type of lesson should be prepared and taught. A good way of revising is to have each member in turn acting as instructor and demonstrator for the various phases of grooming.

OTHER SUBJECTS which could be prepared and taught in similar fashion are: bandaging, clipping and trimming, first aid and surgical bandaging, mucking out, plaiting, mane pulling, tack-cleaning.

SHOEING

'No foot – no horse' is an oft-repeated and wise saying. All members should learn the basic facts about the care of a pony's feet and shoeing, but it is important that they should not go away from a shoeing lesson thinking that they know enough to be critical of a trained farrier's work. If they are genuinely worried about the way in which their pony is being shod, they should seek advice from a knowledgeable person. In time they will have had enough experience to make their own judgment.

The following should have been taught before 'B' Test (15 to 16 years)
(a) Reasons for shoeing (which should include knowledge of the external points of the foot).
(b) How to tell that a pony needs shoeing.
(c) The difference between hot and cold shoeing.
(d) The farrier's tools – their names and functions.
(e) What the farrier has to do:
To remove an old shoe.
To prepare the foot.
To prepare and fit the new shoe.
To nail on and finish off.
(f) How to tell whether a pony has been well shod.
(g) Various types of common shoes, the names of their parts; nails and studs.
(h) The structure of a pony's foot – the names and functions of the various parts.

Allow 45-minute periods for the following lessons:

Preliminary Lesson (covering the 'C' Test syllabus for 10 to 12 year-olds)
(a) Reasons for shoeing.
(b) How to tell that a pony needs shoeing.
(c) Preparation of the feet, explaining the relation to (d) below.
(d) How to tell whether a pony has been well shod.
REQUIREMENTS FOR DEMONSTRATION
☐ A healthy, well-cared for foot.
☐ An overgrown hoof with a too long and turned-up toe (which illustrates the importance of farriers' visits to ponies at grass).
☐ One or more ponies with risen clenches and loose or thin shoes.
☐ A large drawing or diagram of a badly-shod foot and another of a well-shod foot.

Follow-up Lessons (which together cover the 'B' Test syllabus and are suitable for 13 to 15 year-olds)

There is still too much to be taught and too much information to be absorbed for one 45-minute period. Therefore plan two follow-up lessons:

LESSON 1
(a) Revision of preliminary lesson.
(b) Hot and cold shoeing – advantages and disadvantages.
(c) Structure of a pony's foot.
(d) Varieties of common shoes – nails and studs.
REQUIREMENTS
☐ A specimen of a horse's or a pony's hoof and bones, from the fetlock down. A chart showing a pony's lower leg and hoof.
☐ A variety of common shoes, both fore and hind. Nails and studs.

LESSON 2
(a) Revision of previous lessons.
(b) Farrier's tools and their uses.
(c) Removal of an old shoe, then preparing, fitting, and nailing on a shoe.
REQUIREMENTS
☐ A set of farrier's tools in their box.
☐ A quiet horse for a mock shoeing.
   OR:

PRACTICAL DEMONSTRATION
A visit to a forge or – better still, as forges are not designed for class instruction – a visit to a rally or camp by a farrier with a mobile forge. Demonstrations by craftsmen require careful arranging beforehand, so that the group will gain maximum benefit. It is advisable to deal with part of the subject, (a) and (b) above *before* the demonstration, rather than afterwards.

Some farriers are able to explain their work clearly. Others may need help to supplement their commentary. Some may agree to shoe each hoof individually; in this case arrange for a small group to watch one hoof being shod and then change over to another group for the next hoof, rather than having everyone watching at the same time.
REQUIREMENTS
☐ A farrier with his forge and tools.
☐ A supply of water for his bucket.
☐ One pony to be shod.
☐ If visiting the forge, transport for members of the group.

THE FIVE-MINUTE TALK

During the course of a rally the Instructor might decide that the ponies in his group were particularly suitable for teaching a certain topic; or he might have noticed that a certain aspect of stable management was generally sub-standard. Using a break in the mounted lesson, or after lunch, he might take the opportunity to discuss the subject with the riders, using their ponies and equipment. He should give sympathetic help and advice where necessary, and should point out something correct or good about every pony, leaving everyone wiser, and no one demoralised.

Subjects might be:

☐ Types of girths.
☐ Fitting of nosebands (particularly drop nosebands).
☐ Fitting a snaffle bit.
☐ Use of numnahs.
☐ Indication for re-shoeing.
☐ Colours or markings.

OR with older rides:

☐ Fitting curb chains.
☐ Types of saddles.
☐ Respiratory problems.

Although this is no substitute for a class lesson, it is a useful way of pointing out to the group a common weakness or something unusual which would be of interest to them, such as an Appaloosa pony (juniors), a pony shod with three-quarter shoes (middle ride) or a spavin (seniors).

STABLE MANAGEMENT TASKS

This is a way of teaching large numbers at a dismounted rally. It is described on page 19 in Chapter 2.

13 Giving a Lecture

Lectures are used for teaching theoretical subjects such as the principles of feeding and conditioning. Because the subjects will be academic rather than practical, there will be few props, and the Instructor must rely on charts and diagrams to illustrate his talk. The lack of audience participation puts a greater burden on the Instructor who, to maintain interest, will need to rely on his presentation and questions.

STUDY your subject so that you can speak with confidence. Use knowledge acquired from your own experience, from other people, and from books. Know all the different aspects of the subject so that you can discuss it from various angles.

PLAN a lecture of the appropriate length, presented in a logical sequence, as this makes it easier to understand and remember. Be clear and simple.

PREPARE NOTES which can be abbreviated and written on postcards in clearly set-out headings, but have the detail in your mind. Lectures which are read straight from books or scripts can be boring.

MEMORIZE your opening and closing sentences.

Use some visual aids according to the type of lecture, the venue, and the size of the audience. 'The eye is the window to the brain'.
Some suggestions:

(a) Samples of bones, feeds, saddlery or other 'real' items to illustrate your talk. But pass them round only at appropriate times, or they may be distracting.

(b) Diagrams prepared in advance.

(c) Blackboard and chalks.

(d) Viewing aids such as overhead projectors, epidiascopes, etc, are useful, and are often at hand if you are lecturing at a school. They enable you to use pictures or photographs (enlarging if necessary) reflected on to a large screen. They may be used in the same way as a blackboard, but are more impressive. You can make drawings on transparencies either before or during the lecture. One transparency may be placed above another, e.g. the outline of a pony may be saddled up or rugged up.

Whenever possible, *demonstrate* how something should be done. Young members especially like to *watch something* at times during the lecture.

Points to Remember
- Know your subject and prepare it adequately. Most lecturers feel apprehensive before they start; nerves will disappear once you begin.
- Speak slowly and clearly, look at your audience, and ensure that people in the back row can hear.
- Try to avoid mannerisms, which can be distracting.
- Speak with conviction.
- Make their minds work by asking questions during your lecture.
- Leave some time at the end to answer questions, and ask some yourself to bring out specific points.
- Summarize your lecture and offer a conclusion.

14   Using Video

The use of video, both for viewing pre-recorded material and for making recordings, is of great value.

REQUIREMENTS
For Viewing
A television set (preferably colour).
Power source.
A video cassette player and pre-recorded cassette tapes compatible with the player. The vcr will need an extra power outlet.
    If you have a cam-corder with a tv play-back facility you will be able to view your own recorded material.

For Filming
A colour video camera (or a cam-corder) preferably with tripod.
Blank cassette tapes.

The Video Recorder
Video recorders are simple to use. One of their great advantages is that the Instructor can take total control of the programme and repeat any section as many times as he needs to. Other advantages are:
- ☐   Fast re-wind.
- ☐   Slow motion.
- ☐   Static picture.
- ☐   Tapes are re-usable.

NOTE: Before buying or hiring information or teaching-tapes, check that their contents are compatible with Pony Club and British Horse Society teaching methods.

    Preparation is essential. Before showing video tapes, play them through, and decide how to use them. This takes longer than you think!

SUGGESTED USES
- At a dismounted rally with 10 to 12 members of approximately the same age and standard. This is a useful way of including members who do not have their own ponies.
- At a mounted rally or at camp, with the video equipment set up in a horsebox or building, where groups can come in at pre-arranged times with their Instructors.
- As a quiz, with questions compiled in advance.

The Video Camera

The camera can be a most useful addition to any lesson. There are many ways in which it can be used – to improve riding ability, increase knowledge, develop awareness and provide fun.

To gain most benefit from it:

- The activity filmed must be compatible with the standard of the ride.
- Work in small groups.
- The Instructor should not be the camera operator.
- The Instructor should explain to the operator exactly what he hopes to achieve with his lesson, and whether side, front or back views are required.
- The Instructor should stand near to the operator so that all his comments will be picked up on the recorder.
- If any unfortunate incidents should occur which the Instructor would like to have erased the operator must be asked to do this before he continues filming.
- Viewing of the film should be arranged as soon as possible after the lesson that it shows.

WARNINGS

☐ Remember that young children are very excited when they see their pony on the screen for the first time. Several replays may be required before they settle down and attend to the lesson.

☐ Be particularly aware that older, more mature, members are often shocked and demoralized when they see a recording. The image that they have of themselves and their ponies may be very different from what actually appears on the screen. The camera must serve the same purpose as good instruction – and be CONSTRUCTIVE.

SUGGESTIONS FOR FILMING

1. **For all Rides:** *A Jumping Lesson*

- The ride should be filmed while jumping, from the side and the rear. The filming should continue while the Instructor makes comments to each rider after his turn, pointing out his faults and suggesting how these should be corrected.

The lesson should then continue (without filming) until the Instructor is satisfied that every rider shows at least some improvement.

Finally the ride can be re-filmed jumping, as before.

The ride should be shown the film as soon as possible. Each member will then learn, by seeing his own improvement, by listening to the Instructor's comments and by watching the efforts of the other members of the ride. Thus the lesson will be confirmed in a most positive way.

2. For more experienced Members: *A Movement to Ride*

- Once riders have become accustomed to the camera and to their appearance on the screen, the Instructor can use his ingenuity and devise ways of helping them to relate what they *feel* to what they finally *see*.
- While the camera is recording, encourage them to talk about 'how their horse is going'. This helps them to analyse what they have felt and to express themselves clearly. When watching the film they may also check that their comments were relevant.

3. Stable Management

- As an aid to teaching stable management, each ride at camp could prepare a demonstration on pony care. These could then be filmed, and a useful teaching tape made – fun and learning combined.

4. Other Suggestions

- Branch competitions can be filmed, and shown at a fund-raising evening held for parents and friends.
- The Branch can make its own demonstration tapes, with more senior members responsible for the organising. Road safety and countryside studies are among suitable topics.

Further Subjects
For Instruction

15 Countryside Studies and Hunting

An understanding of those subjects should be taught in all branches, regardless of wether or not The Pony Club *Achievement Awards Scheme* is used. Teaching should be according to local conditions, and by knowledgeable local Instructors (who need not be riding Instructors). Occasionally the Instructor and a farmer, or an expert in some aspect of countryside studies, might take the lesson together. The 'expert' can give the main lesson, and the ride Instructor can join in a general discussion or question session, so that the ride learns the subject from different points of view. Such lessons are best given during country rides, when observations can be made at first hand.

Members who hunt should have some knowledge of countryside studies. The importance of teaching courteous behaviour and responsible riding cannot be over-stressed.

Ways of teaching Countryside Studies
1. On instructional hacks (country rides), perhaps in an afternoon at a day rally (see Chapter 2, page 15).
2. On a farm walk, perhaps on a summer evening, followed by a barbecue.
3. During dismounted rallies held at farms, when groups might be taken for a guided tour either on foot or on an open trailer behind a tractor.
4. At lectures, or walks in natural surroundings, under the guidance of experts.
5. As members of a BHS bridlepath working party.

Depending on local conditions, suitable subjects might be:
(a) FARMING How and when it is possible to ride through farmland without causing any damage. Recognising crops, spring and autumn cultivations. Recognising stock and its condition. Maintenance of land; drainage, the dangers of sub-soiling and mole draining to riders. Types of fencing and use of gates. Provision of water for stock.
(b) BRIDLE PATHS How to use them without inconveniencing any other users. The law relating to them.
(c) FORESTRY Rules to observe when riding through woods. Maintenance of trees and paths. Recognizing young trees. Fire precautions.

(D) **FISHING AND SHOOTING** Riding without disturbing game or annoying fishermen. Preservation of game. Rearing seasons. Sporting rights, shooting syndicates, fishing clubs.

(e) **NATURAL HISTORY** Recognizing and being able to name the flora and fauna of the countryside. The characteristics of the seasons.

HUNTING

Hunting conditions vary in different areas, but all members should realise that we hunt by courtesy of landowners and farmers, and that good manners towards all concerned, and particularly the general public, are essential.

Some ways of teaching are:
- [ ] Through practical experience, starting with children's or Pony Club meets, and following the *Hunting Test Syllabus.*
- [ ] At mock hunts. (See Chapter 2, page 16).
- [ ] With lectures, which may include a demonstration of the use of the horn.
- [ ] With videos of hunting which have well-informed commentaries.
- [ ] With lectures or discussions during rallies.
- [ ] With visits to kennels.

Subjects might include:

(a) **THE FOX** His life-style. The need to control numbers, and if hunting is the most humane and practical way.

(b) **THE HUNT** Its Masters, administration, kennels, hunt servants, supporters.

(c) **HOUNDS** Breeding, rearing, walking, entering, exercising, hunting.

(d) **USE OF THE HUNTING WHIP** Cracking it; opening gates; warning hounds away from ponies' heels.

(e) **PREPARATIONS** Fitness of pony. Finding out venue of meet and cost of subscription or cap. Sensible choice of saddlery and clothing. Contents of pockets – money, string, penknife, snacks, etc.

(f) **THE MEET** How to behave, who to identify, who to pay.

(g) **HUNTING LANGUAGE** Expressions used. The horn. Hound language.

(h) **THE HUNTING DAY** Description of particularly interesting hunts which have taken place locally. Imagining situations which might occur concerning hounds, hunt servants, field master, the field. Behaviour in the field.

(i) **THE END OF THE DAY** Etiquette when leaving the field. Riding home. Consideration for pony.

16 Road Safety

The *Road Safety Achievement Badge* must be attained before a 'C' Test certificate can be awarded. After 'C' but before 'B' Members must pass either the BHS Road Safety Test or the Pony Club's Road Safety Test.

EARLY TRAINING
Training must begin at the first opportunity. On enrolment new members should be given a Road Safety booklet, and early rallies should include some instruction on the subject. Every effort should be made to alert parents to the dangers of their children riding on the road. This can be done in a number of ways:
- At parents' meetings, where film or slide packs can be shown.
- Involving parents in teaching the *Highway Code.*
- At field and road tests, with parents acting as helpers.
- At evening quizzes with members.

THE OBJECT OF THE TEST
Riders should be so well schooled in road safety drill and hand signals that these become automatic, leaving the rider free to cope with the pony in traffic or in other difficult situations.

PLANNING INSTRUCTION FOR THE TEST
1. **Mounted**
☐ Know the requirements of the test. (Study the current BHS/Pony Club official Riding and Road Safety booklet and the *Highway Code.*)
☐ Plan a progressive programme of 10- to 15-minute periods, to be fitted into every rally.
OR
☐ Plan a series of road safety rallies.
Either method should end with practice of a field test. Remember to organise any special props – cones, traffic signs, material for marking lines and road junctions, hazards etc. Position them in advance.

2. **Dismounted (Indoors)**
A great deal can be achieved during winter rallies or camp, using the following:
☐ Pony Club video: *Ride Safely.*
☐ Slide pack and talk.
☐ Magnetic board, blackboard or table model – to facilitate discussion of traffic situations which arise while riding on the road.

☐ Quiz.

NOTE: The *Riding and Road Safety Test* is for the rider, not the pony. Though training involves the pony, it is primarily concerned with the rider.

Training should increase the safety of riders on the road, but there can never be any positive guarantee against accidents.

If ponies prove unsuitable to be ridden in the test, parents should be notified. In such cases, the ponies should neither be used for the test nor ridden on the road.

17 Preparing the Ride for Pony Club Competitions

(A) A DRESSAGE TEST (B) SHOW JUMPING (C) RIDING ACROSS COUNTRY

(A) RIDING A DRESSAGE TEST

The prospect of a dressage test can be very alarming to many young riders, and Instructors can help by building up confidence. You should explain that (1) in its simple form dressage is just ordinary training, aimed at producing an obedient pony who goes in a correct way and who is pleasant to ride, and (2) that a dressage test is designed to assess just how successful that training has been. Before attempting a test, members of the ride should be able to perform all the basic movements required, and should be mounted on reasonably obedient ponies. A half-forgotten test on a disobedient pony can easily end in tears and can lead to a lasting dislike of dressage.

Confidence can be built up by:
☐ Learning the test so well that the rider can concentrate on the movements.
☐ Understanding what is required (sometimes outlined in *Notes and Directive Ideas* on the test sheet) so that there is a sense of achievement when movements are performed well.
☐ Realizing that one bad movement or error of course is not the end of the world, as each movement is marked separately.
☐ Practising any movements which may be unfamiliar.
☐ Knowing the procedure at a dressage competition.

Although this lesson can be useful to the more experienced who need to brush up their arena-craft, it is intended mainly for those who are just starting to do dressage tests.

Before the Mounted Lesson

Learning the Test Learning something by memory is an individual problem, and the ability to do so varies widely. This puts severe limitations on achieving it in a ride lesson. The Instructor can help by suggesting aids to memory, and by revising whenever a suitable opportunity presents itself, such as after lunch at a day rally or when sheltering from a sudden downpour of rain.

1. The Instructor can usefully run through the test on a blackboard to make sure that everyone understands what is required.
2. More lasting value will result if each rider is asked to draw an arena on paper and then to trace in the movements.
3. Junior rides will enjoy practising on foot in an arena (approx. 5m × 10m) outlined in chalk on a hard surface.

Checking the Rules Find out which rules are being used, then instruct the members to read the rule book. Check that they know:

☐ The saddlery, dress and equipment that may or may not be used for the test and while working-in.

☐ Whether anyone else is allowed to ride the pony on the day of the competition.

☐ Any other rules which might cause problems.

The Mounted Lesson

Requirements (1) A dressage arena accurately laid out with white boards, letters, and corner markers on a flat place where the going is reasonably good. Try to make the arena as impressive as it will look in the competition itself. Park your car close to the arena at 'C', where the judge's car is usually stationed. (2) An assistant, if there are likely to be more than five members in the ride. You can divide them into two groups. The assistant should be capable of helping a group with basic paces and transitions.

Start the Lesson with the whole ride, as set out in Chapter 5, 'Procedure' (page 34). During the working-in period, riders and ponies should settle and become accustomed to working close to the white boards and the car. Then line up the ride and *explain* that you are going to teach:

(a) What to do at a dressage competition.

(b) How to use the arena correctly.

DISCUSS

(a) On which rein each member will ride before making his entry.

(b) How to ride through the corners without upsetting the pony's balance and rhythm.

(c) How to ride accurately, following the movements laid down in the test, and preparing the pony carefully for the transitions and changes in direction. Having been prepared, transitions written in the test should be made as the *rider* reaches the appropriate marker.

Using the maximum distances between the ponies, the ride can then *practise*:

- Correctly ridden corners.
- Correctly ridden shapes of basic movements in the test, such as circles, changing the rein across the diagonal, or riding on to the centre line.

DISCUSS

(a) Any unusual movement in the test, if necessary by demonstrating its shape on foot.

(b) Any movements which involve lengthening and shortening the reins, or riding with the reins in one hand.

Again, using maximum distances between ponies, the ride should *practise* the above.

Individual practice in the Arena If there are more than five in the ride, take groups of three or four at a time to work in the arena while your assistant helps the others to work on basic paces and transitions near the arena. Divide your time equally between the groups.

Choose your most experienced rider to ride the first movement of the test. He should show:

(a) How to report any changes of pony or rider. This should be to the steward or writer, not to the judge.

(b) How to ride around the outside of the arena until the car-horn or the bell sounds.

(c) A correct turn on to the centre line before entering the arena.

(d) A straight line and a good, still halt.

(e) A correct salute executed without disturbing the pony.

(f) A straight move-off.

While standing in a ride each member might then practise the salute at the halt. Stress again the importance of preparing the ponies in advance for changes in direction or transitions – always thinking and looking ahead. Your next rider can demonstrate the next few movements, and so on, until the end of the test. The rider performing the final movements should also show how to leave the arena.

Riders who are not performing should watch with you, near to 'C', and be encouraged to observe and make comments to you.

MAKE CORRECTIONS at the moment when they are needed. If necessary, revise movements which have caused problems, allowing the riders to perform them again.

TO FINISH discuss turnout and dress as well as a sensible working-in routine to be used on the day of the competition. This will vary according to the individual characteristics of the pony.

Conclusion There will seldom be time for all members to ride the whole test individually during the lesson, and they must be encouraged to practise the movements on their own. Warn them that while they may run through the test a few times on their ponies, they must avoid constant repetition, or the ponies will begin to anticipate.

NOTE: All dressage tests are tests of correct training. Movements performed in Pony Club dressage tests should therefore have been practised at previous Pony Club rallies. The lesson outlined above should consist of revising, practising the movements, and ensuring that every member of the ride has the benefit of working individually, under supervision, in a dressage arena. The use of video can be invaluable if it is presented in a constructive way. (See Chapter 14, page 80).

(B) SHOW JUMPING

The Course

A good show-jumping course consists of a mixture of staircase, upright and parallel fences. Enough equipment should be available to build a good flowing course with turns in both directions and at least one double. The first few fences should be comparatively easy. For junior rides, the first fence should be jumped in the direction of the ride. For junior and middle rides the double should be constructed as two upright fences with 9 to 10 metres (approx. 30 to 33 ft) between them, depending on the height of the fences and the size of the ponies. For advanced rides spread fences may be used in doubles or trebles. The distances should be measured from the last element of the first fence to the first element of the second.

When setting the height of the fences, always err on the side of caution. You can easily enlarge them once the ride has proved that they are too easy.

Have the course ready before the lesson begins. For further information on course building see the British Show Jumping Association's *Notes on Course Building for Show Jumping*.

ASSISTANTS If possible have some dismounted members to help with the fences.

WALKING THE COURSE At competitions, riders must walk the course on foot. At rallies, if the ponies can be left safely it is *preferable* for the ride to inspect the course on foot. Otherwise 'walk' the course with the ride mounted.

DISCUSS:
(a) The track or path to be taken by each pony, a correct line of approach to every fence.
(b) Any undulations in the ground, and the effect on balance and impulsion.
(c) Any other difficulties, such as spread fences after corners, or doubles and trebles.
(d) The importance of knowing the course so well from start to finish that each rider can concentrate on his riding and his pony without fear of going the wrong way.

Preliminary Work on the Flat
After some preliminary exercises, ask each rider to demonstrate the pace in which the course should be jumped. Junior rides should achieve a canter, maintaining the same speed on a circle and a straight line. More advanced rides should achieve an active, balanced, rhythmical canter from which the pony can adjust his stride without breaking his rhythm. The following exercise enables the ride to practise this without jumping the ponies.

Put out six markers as shown in Fig. 27.

Tell each rider to perform a circle of about 20 metres, followed by a straight line of about 60 metres, followed by another circle the same size as the first, followed by a returning straight line. Working one at a time, the ride could:
1. Practise riding the shape of the exercise in trot.
2. Ride it in canter, keeping a constant rhythm.

Fig. 27 An exercise on the flat.

3. Proceed as in (2) but count aloud the strides between the markers and ask for some stronger strides on the returning line, which should also be counted. The return will probably be made with one or two strides less.

4. As (3) but ask for shorter than normal strides on the returning line. The circles should always be performed at the basic jumping canter, which is active and from which the individual pony can easily lengthen or shorten his stride. The exercise should be carried out on both reins. Some show-jumping ponies shorten their strides by swinging their hindquarters sideways. Their riders should attempt to control the quarters and to ride the ponies straight. Depending on the standard of the ride, the exercise may be varied. Suggest that the ride pretends that there is a large parallel fence half-way down the straight line. This would necessitate asking for stronger strides on the last quarter of the circle so that the pace is established before the mock fence. (Do not mark the exact position, or the riders might spoil the exercise by abruptly trying to 'find a stride'.) *Or* pretend that there is a large gate a quarter of the way down the straight line. This would need to be 'jumped' from a short active canter, which would give the pony time to see the fence and judge his stride ready for take-off.

Jumping the Course in Sections

If a practice fence is available, it may be preferable to work the more advanced ride over it and then over the whole course, as in a competition. With a less experienced ride or a ride of young horses, it helps to jump the course in sections.

Each pony should jump the first fence, which will be small and simple. The rest of the course may be tackled one or two fences at a time. The riders' positions and the methods of approach, jump, and recovery should be corrected if necessary. Sluggish ponies may need leads to get them going. The double may cause problems: make it simple at first, and ensure that timid ponies have a 'carrot' about twenty metres away on the landing side.

Jumping the Whole Course

- Discuss the rules and methods used in judging show jumping.
- Remind the ride of the points discussed and the plans made while walking the course.
- Emphasize the importance of executing the plan accurately (riding the corners correctly, etc.).
- Have a 'start', a 'finish', and a whistle or some signal for the riders

to begin. The ride will then become familiar with show jumping procedure.

Next, tell each rider in turn to jump the course. While the course is being jumped, stress the importance of rhythm, balance and speed control throughout the whole round. The rhythm should remain constant. Correct those riders who lose the rhythm on the corners while they take a rest. Although sluggish ponies may have to be ridden hard at their fences, the average pony moving with sufficient impulsion will jump better if he is not pulled almost to a standstill and then suddenly bustled at the fence for the last three strides.

Point out mistakes to the rest of the ride as they occur. After each round discuss how successfully the course was ridden. Did the rider stay on the track as planned? Was he able to maintain rhythm, balance and impulsion? Why were fences knocked down? Did the rider take away the pony's concentration or unbalance him by looking back to see if a pole had fallen at the previous fence? Did the pony run out at the double because the rider failed to ride to the centre of the second (final) element?

The Second Round
Any riders who had difficulty the first time round should jump the same course again – trying, with the Instructor's help, to correct their mistakes. For those who had little difficulty, the fences may be raised and made wider according to the ability of the ride.

The Timed Jump-off
Use a shortened course with turns both ways. Explain that control is essential and that the quickest round will not be achieved by the rider whose pony gallops fastest, but by the rider who rides the neatest track while maintaining rhythm and balance at as fast a speed as possible.

With impetuous competition ponies it may be unwise to practise this, as unless the fences are high and impressive, any increase in speed may result in careless jumping. Suggest that their riders practise riding a careful neat track. This will leave the ponies settled in their minds for future competitions.

With most rides the shortened course may be jumped against the clock, the Instructor timing each round. Riders who achieve good results can finish, and begin to cool off their ponies. Those who do not manage to ride neatly and accurately should immediately try another round, after discussing their problems with the Instructor. In almost every case this extra round will be better and faster. Even sluggish ponies who do not like jumping become more enthusiastic, while their riders feel a distinct sense of achievement. This is a good note on which to end a lesson. The ride should walk on a long rein around the fences to cool off the ponies. NOTE: The less controllable show-jumping ponies often have exceptional natural jumping ability which has been over-exploited, their early training having been neglected. Their riders are brave, but have little control. Therefore if such a pony begins to settle and 'listen' to his rider, the rider must improve himself and give the correct aids, or the pony will misunderstand and may start to refuse. Beware of making radical changes to successful partnerships during the competition season.

The thinking rider will quickly realize the long-term importance of improving his riding.

(C) RIDING ACROSS COUNTRY

General Considerations
Mention of going across country conjures up visions of galloping over fields with successive lines of beautiful, straightforward fences, and hounds in front. Teaching cross-country riding is a very different matter. The rider must be taught:

(a) To ride at a specific speed in cold blood away from and towards the rest of the ride.

(b) To jump straightforward fences at a basic cross-country speed, and tricky fences from slow speeds.

(c) To ride on an accurate line towards, over, and away from a fence. (To practise this, see Exercise 8 on page 70.)

(d) To jump related fences on the flat and on different ground levels. (See 'Doubles', pages 68.)

(e) To jump on gradients (see page 69) and over drop fences.

(f) To jump ditches and water.

(g) To ride through water.

Correct riding with a secure position is essential across country. The rider must be able to achieve a controlled, accurate approach, and must not fall off if the pony makes an awkward jump or pecks on landing. Begin in a simple way: it is impossible to turn an average 'C' ride into an inter-branch team at the drop of a hat. However, aim to improve the control and rhythm of the paces and by the end of the lesson to increase the confidence of each pony and rider.

Start with warming-up exercises on the flat, and then find an easy fence over which the ponies can stretch their muscles and the ride can be assessed.

Speed Control
The ride should learn to jump a straightforward, solid-looking fence at each individual pony's optimum cross-country pace. To practise this, the ride should line up well on the landing side of the fence. Each rider should make a long approach and should continue on the landing side in the same rhythmical cross-country pace. Next the ride should practise jumping a low fence from a trot with a short approach, then turning either way immediately after the fence.

The Course
At competitions, the course must be walked by riders on foot, but at rallies, if a course is available it can be 'walked' by the ride on their ponies. All fences can then be discussed and practised over as you go along. It sometimes helps to give timid ponies a lead. Remember that because of differences in type and ability, the ponies may tackle some fences in different ways, choosing whichever way is easiest for them.
    At each fence discuss:
(a) The line of approach.
(b) The speed of approach and how far away that speed should be established.
(c) The take-off and landing zones.
(d) The line of the recovery stride.
(e) The impulsion needed in the recovery stride. (This is especially important in an uphill combination.)
(f) The line and speed to be taken towards the next fence.
(g) The importance of maintaining contact and of moving confidently forward in the final stage before take-off: even if the fence is a 2-metre drop approached in walk!
(h) How to tackle multiple fences. Look at the positions of the flags and the different ways in which the fences may be jumped. Consider this with each individual rider, as the fences may pose different problems for each of them, and different lines of approach, jump and recovery may be chosen.

Fences with Obscure Landings
These include obstacles which entail jumping from light to dark, into shadows or woods, and 'into space'. They often cause ponies to refuse.
    Before expecting a pony to take off it is necessary to allow him to see what is on the landing side. This is achieved by making a slow approach but with strong rhythm and impulsion, either in trot or slow canter. In this way he has time to see where he is going and still has the impetus to go there.

95

Ditches

These often cause problems, especially if rider and pony look down into the bottom of the ditch. If the ditch is in front of the fence, rider and pony should concentrate firmly on the *fence*. If it is just a plain ditch they should concentrate on the *landing side*. If the pony shies and decreases the speed, his rider must be quick to maintain impulsion. If his hocks are engaged he can still jump the ditch however slowly he is going. See also 'Ditches' page 69.

Jumping into Water

Only practise this if the water is shallow, has a sound bottom, and is far too wide (over 8 metres) for the ponies to jump. Walk the ride through the water and allow the ponies to stand and splash a little until they are completely familiar with it. Then progress slowly, from walking and then trotting off the bank into the water, to jumping a small fence.

In competitions water should be approached in the same way as for 'Fences with Obscure Landings' (described above) except that if the fence is small the speed may be slower. If there is a steep approach or a large drop into the water, it might be safer to walk.

Corner Fences (Fig. 28).

When built on flat terrain, it is possible to negotiate these in three different ways:

LINE 1 One non-jumping stride between the elements. This line should always be chosen unless the rider is capable of riding on a completely accurate line through the obstacle.

LINE 2 Both elements cleared in one jump. The approach should be on a line to an imaginary fence which bisects the angle made by the two elements. It is unwise to choose this approach if the pony is likely to run out or to veer sideways as he jumps. Accuracy is essential.

LINE 3 'Bouncing' over the obstacle. Plan the line according to the 'bounce' distance which each pony takes when schooling over bounce fences of this height. If such schooling has not been carried out, this plan is not advisable.

Corner fences can be in many different forms. The lines shown in Fig. 28 are not always straight, and the angle of the corners will vary from being very narrow and inviting, to being too wide to jump. Check the position of the flags, consider all the possibilities, and judge each case on its own merits.

Tantivies

These are useful for encouraging the confidence of both rider and pony.

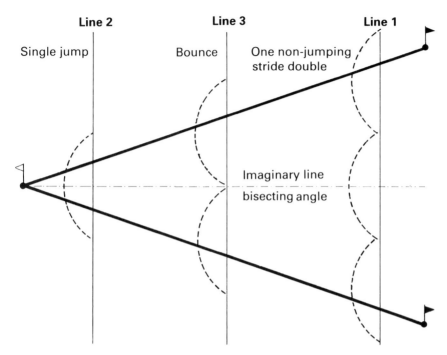

Line 2   **Line 3**   **Line 1**

Single jump   Bounce   One non-jumping stride double

Imaginary line bisecting angle

Fig. 28 Three different ways to jump a corner fence.

If the Instructor has a suitable horse he may act as 'field-master', leading the ride round the cross-country course. Otherwise the ride may be sent round in groups, pairs or singly, according to how they will manage best. The Instructor should be careful to maintain control and to keep the ride in sight at all times. He should never take the risk of allowing riders to jump too fast into quarries, combinations, or other tricky fences – which could cause horrific falls. Riders whose ponies are inclined to run away should be sent singly; and the faint-hearted – whether rider or pony – should be sent with a combination who will provide a satisfactory lead.

Determination
The tantivy can be used as fun to finish off a junior lesson, but for the more advanced it should only be used as a means to an end, as they should learn to make their ponies go in cold blood – i.e. without the encouragement of company. This takes far more skill and determination, and teaches the important lesson that no sensible pony goes across country alone without clear, concise, and emphatic guidance from the rider.

Conditioning and Fitness

It should be made clear that ponies need to be considerably fitter for cross-country events than for normal hacking. During the cross-country lesson, time should be taken to discuss suitable training programmes, thereby ensuring that the ponies are adequately prepared for any strenuous events for which they are entered.

Cooling Off

As always, the lesson should end on a happy note, perhaps with the ride having satisfactorily jumped one or two straightforward fences. As the ponies will have been galloping, they should be dismounted and led with girths loosened and stirrups up, until they are dry and settled. The Instructor should ensure that the riders understand how to look after their ponies both before and after they have been galloping. It is important to discuss the special care needed in feeding and watering during training and on the day of the competition.

For The More Experienced Instructor

18 School Movements Performed in Various Ways – Formation Riding

School movements performed in various ways under a competent Instructor are interesting and fun for the ride. They may also be used in a suitable order to produce a formation ride. First make sure that you can control the ride, as described in Chapter 4 (page 26).

Secondly, practise new movements with matches on a tray before trying them out at the rally. Use one match per rider.

Most movements may be performed by the ride in the following ways:
'In single file'.
'In succession'.
'By rides'.
'Double ride'.
'Whole ride'.

'In single file', *'in succession'*, and *'whole ride'* are explained in Chapter 4 on page 28.

Before being able to carry out more complicated movements with your ride you must know, and the ride must understand, the following:

Numbering means that each member of the ride calls out his number. The words of command are: *'Ride from the front, over your inside shoulder – number'*. The leading file turns his head to the inside and says *'One'*, whereupon the rider behind him turns his head and says *'Two'*, the next *'Three'*, and so on, until the rear of the ride is reached. It is sometimes advisable to repeat this.

Proving means that each rider 'proves' that he has memorized his number. When his number is called he responds by transferring his reins and whip to his outside hand, then raises his inside arm, straight, forward, and level with his shoulder.

Dividing into rides (for work by rides) means dividing the class, after numbering, into equal groups. Words of command might be *'Numbers 1 to 4 are Number 1 ride. Numbers 5 to 8 are Number 2 ride'*. Alternatively, the riders may be numbered from the front in fours (or twos, threes or fives).

Double Ride means that the ride is divided into two from the front, odd numbers in one ride and even numbers in the other. Odd numbers are responsible for the pace, and even numbers for the dressing. Each ride follows its own leading file.

Dressing means keeping in line or in position during a movement *'Dressing by the left'* means that every rider glances to his left and keeps in line with the rider at the left end of the row. Each rider is responsible for keeping his own dressing. Unless commanded otherwise, dressing is always carried out by keeping in line with the riders on the side towards which the turn is made.

Manège or School It is usual to use the word 'school' when giving commands (e.g. 'Turning across the school'). 'School' is therefore used in this chapter when discussing the control of the ride, although it is recognized that the riding area would generally be an outdoor manège.

NOTE: When working in the school in opposite directions, riders should pass left hand to left hand.

WORKING BY RIDES

- Number the whole ride from the front and divide it into smaller rides: e.g. a ride of 9 into 3 rides of 3; a ride of 8 into 2 rides of 4.
- Check that everyone knows to which ride they belong.
- When performing a movement by rides each member of the named ride obeys the executive command at the same moment and keeps his dressing from the rider on the side to which they have turned: i.e. if the ride is turned to the right, dressing is kept from the rider on the right.
- When manoeuvring by rides with the riders coming towards you, watch where the leading rider of the first ride moves off the track. Then time your executive commands to subsequent rides so that their leaders leave the track at the same place.
- If the rides are going away from you, check that the rear file of each ride turns in the same place.
- If you turn the second and subsequent rides too early, the riders will be baulked when they reach the track. If you turn them too late, gaps will appear between the rides.

Now try:

Turning by Rides (Fig. 29)

Turns across the school should be ordered as the rides approach the end of the long side. The riders in each ride turn on command, simultaneously, staying on the same rein and having plenty of the next long side to ride down after they have turned. Note that Number 4 in each ride becomes the leading file. To bring back Number 1 to the front, turn by rides again.

COMMAND *'By rides, turning across the school, Number 1 ride turn . . . Number 2 ride turn, etc.'*

Turning across the School with a Change of Rein (Fig 30)

These should be ordered as soon as the first ride is on the long side so that there is plenty of long side left after changing the rein.

COMMAND *'By rides, turning across the school to change the rein, Number 1 ride turn . . . Number 2 ride turn, etc.'*

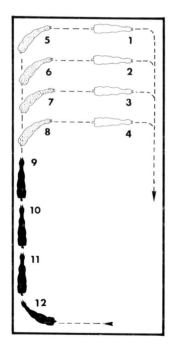

Fig. 29 By rides, turning across the school.

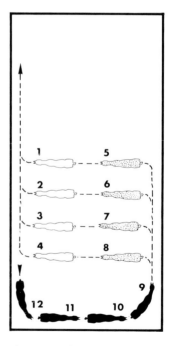

Fig. 30 By rides, turning across the school to change the rein.

102

DOUBLE RIDE WORK

Preferably this should be carried out in a larger manège of 60 × 30 metres.

- Select two competent riders to be Numbers 1 and 2.
- Number the ride from the front.
- Check that the riders know their numbers.
- Turn the ride in single file down the centre.
- Before Number 1 reaches the end of the school, instruct the odd numbers to go on to the left (or right) rein, and the even numbers to go on to the right (or left) rein.
- The pace is set by the Number 1 rider. Riders must keep double distance from each other. They must not close up. The even numbers dress opposite the double distance between the odd numbers: i.e. Number 4 dresses opposite the gap between Numbers 3 and 5. (Fig 31a).
- When riders pass those in the other ride they should pass left hand to left hand, leaving a definite space between the rides (Fig. 31b).
- The ride on the outside has further to go than the ride on the inside. The speed must be regulated accordingly.

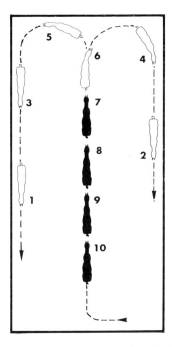

Fig. 31a Dividing into a double ride.

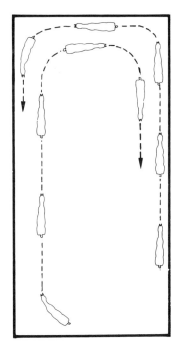

Fig. 31b Double ride passing left hand to left hand.

- When turning the rides down the centre line in pairs, even numbers must dress alongside their odd numbers: i.e. 1 and 2 together (Fig. 31c).

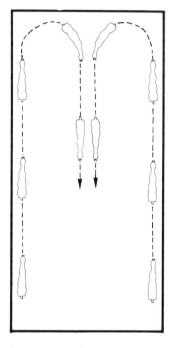

Fig. 31c Double ride turning down the centre in pairs.

A DRILL RIDE

The following drill ride is fun for everyone. Leading-rein rides can perform it at the walk.

Turn the ride down the centre line in pairs. (See Fig. 31c).

To bring the ride down the centre in fours:

COMMAND *'First pair to the left, second pair to the right'*.

RESULT As the pairs reach the opposite end of the manège they turn alternately left and right.

Then, as they are halfway up the manège:

COMMAND *'By fours down the centre'*.

RESULT As each pair reaches the centre marker they turn, as fours, down the centre.

This may continue until eights or sixteens come in a line down the centre, at which point the Instructor might command a halt and salute.

To revert to a single line from fours:

As the fours proceed down the centre line:

COMMAND *'Pairs to the left and right'.*

RESULT At the end of the manège the two on the left turn left, the two on the right turn right.

As the pairs are half-way up the side:

COMMAND *'By pairs down the centre'.*

RESULT The left pair will turn first, with the right pair turning in behind them; then the next left pair, and so on.

As the pairs proceed down the centre:

COMMAND *'Odd numbers turn left, even numbers turn right'.*

RESULT The ride follows the command.

COMMAND *'In single file down the centre, form a single ride'.*

RESULT The ride turns into its original order. Make sure that Number 1 rider knows that he must turn in front of Number 2 rider on to the centre line.

COMMAND *'Leading file on the left (or right) rein.'*

RESULT The ride follows the leading file on to the outer track.

NOTE: Before carrying out the above in trot or canter, consider the size of the manège, the size of the ponies, and the difficulty of the turns.

VARIOUS WAYS OF PERFORMING SIMPLE MOVEMENTS
INCLINING ACROSS THE SCHOOL

The rein is changed by inclining diagonally.

1. In Single File

The ride moves across the diagonal line from the first quarter-marker on one long side to the last quarter-marker on the other.

COMMAND *'In single file, inclining across the school, leading file – inwards incline.'*

RESULT On the word 'incline', the leading file moves off the track. The rest of the ride follows in single file, starting the movement at the same point as the leading file. (Fig. 32a).

2. By Rides

COMMAND *'By rides, inclining across the school, Number 1 ride – inwards incline'.*

RESULT On the word 'incline', each member of Number 1 ride moves simultaneously off the track. The dressing should be taken from the leading file. The shoulders of all the riders should be in line (Fig. 32b).

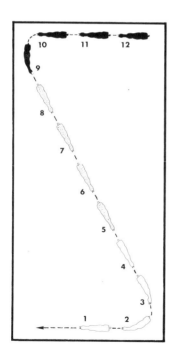

Fig. 32a In single file, inclining across the school.

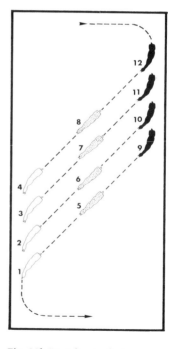

Fig. 32b By rides, inclining across the school.

3. Whole Ride

Only possible if the manège is long enough and there is a suitable number of riders.

COMMAND *'Whole ride, inclining across the school – inwards incline'.*

RESULT On the word 'incline' every member of the ride moves off the track.

4. Double Ride

For this to succeed the rides must have kept their distances and dressing correctly. (See 'Double Ride Work', page 103).

COMMAND *'Rides inclining across the school, leading files – inwards incline.'* Give the executive command as the leading files approach the quarter-markers.

RESULT The two leading files (Numbers 1 and 2) move off the track, followed in single file by their respective rides. The rides cross in the centre of the manège ('Scissors'). See Fig. 32c.

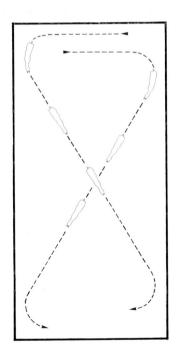

Fig. 32c Double ride inclining across the school.

INDIVIDUAL CIRCLES

1. In Single File

This is not always a satisfactory exercise, as the leading, and perhaps the second, file will describe the circle while the other ponies follow, without much effort from their riders.

A much better exercise is:

2. Circling in Succession

COMMAND *'In succession, large circle to take the rear. Leading file – circle – next – next – next'*, and so on.

RESULT On the word 'Circle' the leading file moves off the track and describes a large circle, planning it so that he rejoins the track at the rear of the whole ride.

FOUR WAYS OF PERFORMING SMALL CIRCLES

Small circles can be performed (1) in single file, (2) by rides, (3) by the whole ride and (4) in double rides.

COMMAND **'In single file,** *circle on to the centre line and return to the track, leading file circle'.*

RESULT In single file the ride describes a semi-circle on to the centre line (between A and C) and proceeds (towards A or C) until the given command 'Away', when, remaining in single file, the ride describes another semi-circle back on to the track and goes large on the original rein.

COMMAND *'**By rides,** circle on to the centre line and return to track. Number 1 ride commence'* ... *'Number 2 ride commence'* ... etc.

RESULT On command, each ride describes a semi-circle to the centre line and proceeds in single file on the centre line until commanded 'Away'. Then each ride describes another semi-circle back on to the track and goes large on the original rein. (Fig. 33).

As explained fully on page 101 every ride must circle at the same place.

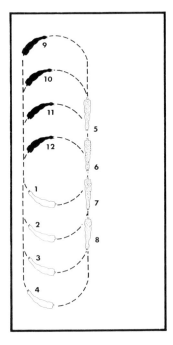

Fig. 33 By rides, circling on to the centre line.

COMMAND *'**Whole ride,** circle on to the centre line and return to track, ride circle'*.

RESULT Every rider simultaneously describes a semi-circle on to the centre line and proceeds in single file until commanded 'Away'. Then each rider describes another semi-circle back on to the track and goes large on the original rein.

DOUBLE RIDE The ride will have been divided into a double ride. The leading files will be nearing the end of the long sides when the executive command is given.

COMMAND *'**Double ride,** circle on to the centre line and return to track. Rides circle'.*

RESULT The rides circle in towards each other, slotting into the gaps (the double distance) when they reach the centre line (Fig. 34a). The rides proceed in single file on the centre line until the command 'Away'. They then turn in alternate directions, describing semi-circles and returning to their respective long sides, going large in their original directions (Fig. 34b).

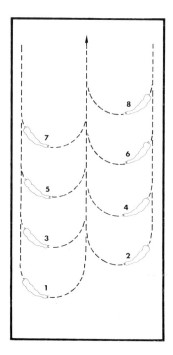

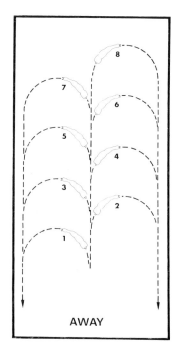

Fig. 34a Double ride circling on to the centre line.

Fig. 34b Double ride circling on to the centre line (away).

The rides can be told to form pairs on the centre line. The commands are the same as those above, but even numbers must have been told to draw level with odd numbers before the movement begins. (Figs. 35a and 35b).

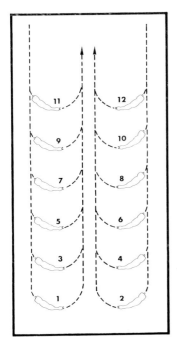

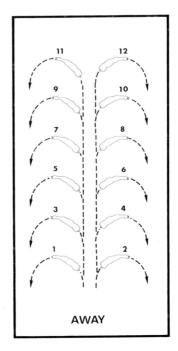

Fig. 35a The alternative way of 'Double ride circling on to the centre line.'

Fig. 35b The alternative way of 'Double ride circling on to the left line (away).'

HALF FIGURE-OF-EIGHT

Preliminary commands (1) 'In single file'. (2) 'By rides'. (3) 'Whole ride'. (4) 'Double ride'.

EXECUTIVE COMMAND: *'Leading file',* (OR *'Number 1 ride'*, OR *'Double ride')* – *'Commence.'*

RESULT The ride proceeds as in the exercise for 'Small Circles', but on the command 'Away' the rider makes a semi-circle back to the track on the opposite side, going large on the other rein (i.e. he first circles right and then left). The movement is shown 'in single file' (Fig. 36a) and 'by rides' (Fig. 36b).

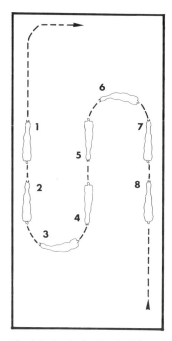

Fig. 36a In single file, half figure-of-eight.

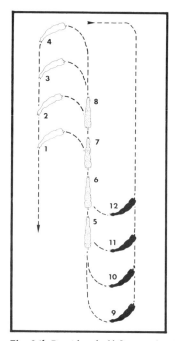

Fig. 36b By rides, half figure-of-eight.

Finally, to revise:
FIVE WAYS OF PERFORMING 'TURNING ACROSS THE SCHOOL'

Fig. 37a. *'In single file, turning across the school – leading file, turn'.*

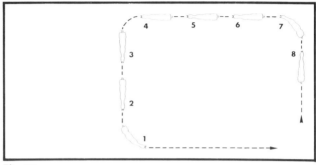

Fig. 37a

Fig. 37b. *'By rides, turning across the school – Number 1 ride, turn'.*

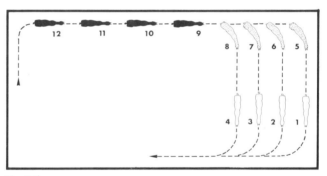

Fig. 37b

Fig. 37c. *'Whole ride, turning across the school – whole ride, turn'.*

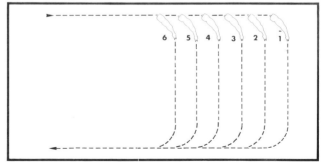

Fig. 37c

Fig. 37d. *'In succession, turning across the school to join the rear of the ride – leading file, turn'.*
Give the executive commands 'Leading file turn – next – next', choosing moments when each rider will be able to join the rear of the ride without breaking his pony's rhythm. By the time the leading file in Fig. 37d rejoins the ride, he will arrive, at the correct distance, as rear file.

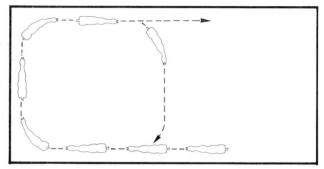

Fig. 37d

Fig. 37e. *'Double ride turning across the school inwards turn'.* Time the words of command so that the turn is made when the rides are on opposite sides of the manège. Both rides turn off the track simultaneously and the riders pass each other as they cross the centre line.

A halt ordered on the centre line ensures control.

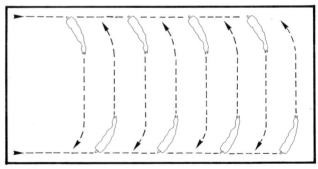

Fig. 37e

Points to remember

- Explain any new exercises carefully. Demonstrate them if necessary, then ask if the ride understands.
- New exercises should be ridden and established at the walk before attempting them at the trot (or perhaps, later, at canter).
- It is better for the ride to perform simple exercises well than to be confused with work which is too complicated.
- Each rider should ride forward with thought and care, to keep his place in the ride, and to help the other riders to keep their places.
- Encourage members to work on their ponies individually.
- Formation riding can be hard work for the average pony and should not be continued for too long.
- Double ride work is an enjoyable way of finishing off a lesson.
- Practised, and set to music, a series of movements can make an impressive display or formation ride.
- If things go wrong, don't panic. Halt the ride, reorganize, and try again at the walk.

TRICYCLING

Tricycling provides a large class with the security of single file conditions and the advantages of individual practice. The ride can carry out quite complicated movements without any command from the Instructor. Although most valuable when taking a large group of members, it can be interesting and fun for all rides.

1. The command 'Commence tricycling' is given as the leader approaches the short side of the manège.
2. In the corner, the leader turns in the normal way, remaining on the outer track, but the second and third riders do not follow. They turn *with* the leader at the same time, and cross the short side of the manège shoulder to shoulder.
3. The next right or left turn brings them once more into single file in reverse order.

Fig. 38 shows three positions of the white horse, the grey, and the black while tricycling around the manège.

The changing from single file on the long side to three abreast on the short side is automatic, and is repeated by the riders until they are told to stop tricycling.

Once the ride has grasped the basic principle and has negotiated the first turn across the side of the school, the groups of three, and each rider's position in his group, will have been established without the need to number the ride off 'by threes'.

115

Fig. 38 Three positions of the white horse, the grey, and the black while tricycling.

All groups of three follow exactly in the tracks of the first three; i.e. in the first corner, Number 4 rides into the corner and turns, remaining on the outer track, while Number 5 and 6 turn alongside him. This is repeated throughout the ride.

Having established his position in the group of three, each rider will notice that he follows the line of the rider in the same relative position of the group in front, i.e. Numbers 2, 5 and 8 will follow on in the same tracks (with plenty of room between them).

Once the ride has mastered tricycling around the manège (riding down the long side in single file and across the short side three abreast) other movements can be introduced. The ride might perform inclining (Fig. 39a), large circles (Fig. 39b), half figures-of-eight (Fig. 39c), serpentines, loops, and many others. The leading three choose among themselves the direction or movement. The Instructor's commands should be kept to a minimum. Tricycling may be performed to music.

Points to remember
- Every rider must concentrate, must think ahead, and must follow exactly in the track of his corresponding number.
- His corresponding number is *never* the one just in front; he must follow the *third* horse in front.
- In turning across the manège the dressing is taken from the inside rider.
- The inside rider must adjust his pace so that having turned across the manège he fits in again at the correct distance behind the group in front. (He is now the leader of his own group).
- Riders in each group must always be the same distance from the long sides of the manège as their group leader; they turn away together, and must therefore arrive together at the side. This is particularly important when moving across the manège as in the change of rein.

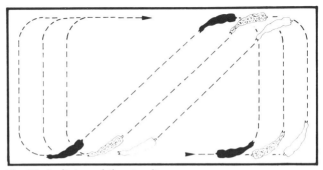

Fig. 39a Inclining while tricycling.

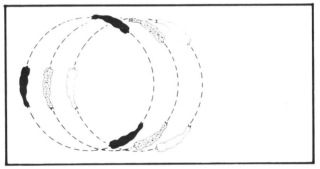

Fig. 39b Circling while tricycling.

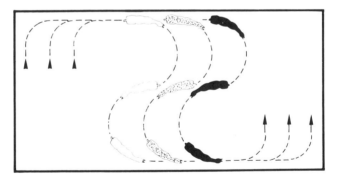

Fig. 39c Half figures-of-eight while tricycling.

The advantage of tricycling is that it enables the Instructor to concentrate on the riding, but he should avoid making too many comments during the exercise.

The same system may be used for *bicycling*, when two riders, instead of three, perform, as in tricycling.

PRODUCING A FORMATION RIDE

Most of the movements described in this chapter are suitable for inclusion in a formation ride.

Consider:

- [ ] The numbers of riders.
- [ ] The size of the ponies.
- [ ] The colours of the ponies.
- [ ] The size of the manège.
- [ ] Where the spectators will be.
- [ ] Where the salute should be made.
- [ ] The time allowed.

Using movements suitable for the standard of the ride, write down the correct commands for your formation ride. Prepare suitable music and equipment. The volume and tone should be reasonable. Scottish reels, Irish jigs, and Country and Western music are generally suitable.

Consider what everyone will wear. Matching sweaters are effective.

If possible, use a member of your ride to try the movements and to check how long the display will take.

With the Ride

1. Arrange the riders in an appropriate order.
2. Practise the ride at the walk, teaching a few movements at a time.
3. Go through the whole series at the walk.
4. Practise at the appropriate paces.
5. Try it with the music.

Simple exercises performed well and accurately look better than complicated ones performed badly.

To ensure a successful performance the Instructor must ALWAYS COMMAND THE RIDE.

19 Trotting-Poles and Gymnastic Jumping Exercises

Trotting-poles and gymnastic exercises are useful training aids in teaching the horse and adult rider to jump. They are most valuable during private lessons, Pony Club camps or regular lessons with horses and riders who are known to you. It should be said, however, that since gymnastic exercises require fences set at closely related distances, the problems of using them at working rallies sometimes outweighs the advantages.

They are not suitable for the child's first pony who, with his novice rider, will hardly manage enough impulsion to negotiate a line of related fences correctly. The average Pony Club ride consists of ponies of different types with varying lengths of stride. The distances between poles must be correct for each pony, or irreparable damage – both physical and psychological – may ensue. Valuable time will also be lost adjusting the distances. Nevertheless, as long as the ride is well enough advanced to control the speed and tempo of the trot, useful lessons with trotting-poles may be given. Should conditions be right, and enough time and equipment available, gymnastic jumping exercises might then be performed. An enclosed area is preferable for jumping, and is essential for work without holding the reins.

Trotting-Poles

Trotting over a series of poles on the ground is an extension of correct work on the flat and is useful because:

For the Pony

- It improves the trot by increasing the activity of the shoulders and hindquarters.
- It regulates the length and rhythm of the stride, thus improving the balance.
- As the pony looks down to see and avoid the poles he is encouraged to stretch and round his back.

For the Rider

- It teaches the feel and tempo of a steady, rhythmical active trot.
- It improves his position and balance as he learns to stay in harmony with his pony.
- It teaches a correct approach, not interfering with the pony except to maintain a rhythmical trot on the correct line of approach.
- It teaches the feel of a light contact with the pony's mouth, which should be maintained at all times, especially when the pony takes the bit and stretches his head out and down. The rider should allow the pony to take this extra rein without moving his weight in the saddle.

Riders who have difficulty in maintaining their positions should use neckstraps, or they will upset the balance and rhythm of their ponies. The neckstrap should be fitted so that it is conveniently placed for the rider to hold without having to move his weight.

Work over trotting-poles is generally carried out at rising trot, and should be performed on either diagonal. More advanced rides may use sitting trot.

Equipment
A minimum of four poles will be needed; but with five trotting-poles, two pairs of stands, and seven additional poles, a suitable combination of trotting-poles and fences may be built if required.

Positioning the Equipment
Position the trotting-poles alongside a hedge or fence or the wall of an indoor school. This will help to keep the ponies straight.

Method
The ride should first walk and then take rising trot over a single pole with the Instructor watching to see that each pony negotiates the pole calmly and without breaking the rhythm (Fig. 40a).

The ride may then trot over the poles with two trotting strides between them (2.5m or approx. 8ft for ponies). (Fig. 40b).

Fig. 40a One pole.   **Fig. 40b** Two poles.

Never trot the ride over two poles at a trotting stride (1.25m or approx. 4ft apart) as the ponies might try to jump the two poles.

Next, add a third pole midway between the first two, thus giving three poles at trotting distance. (Fig. 40c).

The Instructor must watch carefully to see that the distances between the poles are correct for the ponies, as although he may start with a measured 1.25m distance between each pole the distances will probably need adjusting, so that they are correct enough for the ride to trot over easily. Poles which are knocked out of place must be put back.

Having established that the distance between the poles is comfortable for the ponies in the ride, add a fourth pole, about 1.25m after the third (Fig. 40d). Further poles added at correct distances help to develop rhythm and balance.

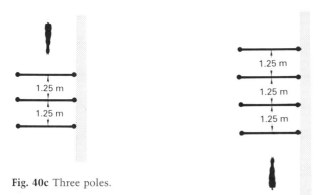

Fig. 40c Three poles.   **Fig. 40d** Four poles

Change the rein frequently. At this stage the poles may be approached in either direction.

If you have time, remove one of the inside poles to see whether the ponies maintain their rhythm and stride when there is a pole missing. Then replace it.

Each rider should try to maintain the rhythm of the trot through the poles and on round the manège.

Trotting-Poles with One Jump

If the ride is negotiating the trotting-poles satisfactorily and if the same distances between the poles are correct for all the ponies in the ride, a small jump may be built about 2.5 metres (8ft) from the last of the four trotting-poles (Fig. 41).

Use a substantial pole, with crossed poles or a diagonal pole underneath it, and a take-off pole on the ground a few inches in front. Measure from the last of the trotting-poles to the take-off pole.

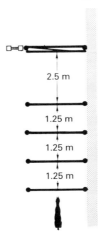

Fig. 41 Four trotting-poles and one jump.

Each pony in turn should trot over the poles and jump the fence at the end.

Check that they take off from both hind legs in unison; a sign that the hocks are correctly engaged. The riders should sit quietly and in harmony with the movement of the ponies.

Sometimes quite startling improvement can be made by taking the riders' minds off the actual jump. Getting them to sing, or to concentrate on some object ahead, can reduce the tension transmitted from them to their ponies, and the wildest pony will often settle and perform calmly.

Trotting-Poles with Two or Three Jumps

If the above-mentioned exercise is performed satisfactorily a second fence may be built (about 5 metres or 16ft, for ponies) away from the first fence. (Fig. 42).

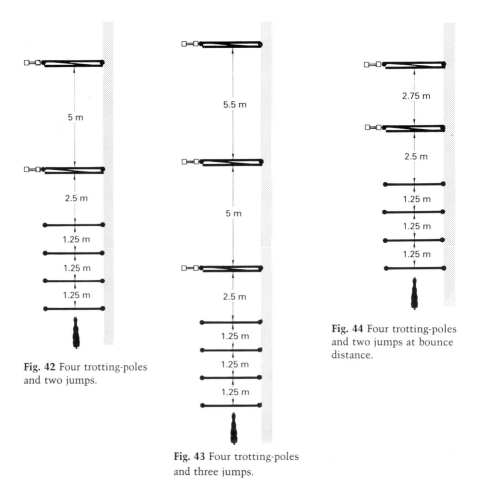

Fig. 42 Four trotting-poles and two jumps.

Fig. 43 Four trotting-poles and three jumps.

Fig. 44 Four trotting-poles and two jumps at bounce distance.

The ponies should trot over the poles, jump the first fence, take one canter stride, and jump the second fence. If they manage this calmly and fluently, and if the area is big enough, a third, slightly higher, fence may be added about 5.5 metres (18ft) from the second (Fig. 43).

The distance between the second and third fence should be slightly longer than the distance between the first and second fence, as by then the ponies will have established a stronger canter rhythm. The distances between the fences are approximate. Use your judgment to adjust them until they are correct for the ponies.

This permutation, with two, three or more fences, may be used as a base for many valuable exercises. Once the ponies have trotted over the poles – provided the tempo and rhythm are maintained and the distances are correct – there is little to go wrong. Thus ponies and riders learn to relax during the approach and over the fences; and the riders develop feel and appreciation for the movement and power of their ponies.

Physical Exercises for Riders while Jumping
Once the ponies are performing fluently over the previous line of poles and fences, the riders may perform exercises to improve their positions, such as: each rider ties his reins in a knot. He then trots over the poles, and as the pony jumps the first fence the rider loses the reins and either puts his hands on his hips, strokes the pony's neck, or makes any other movement designed to help his particular problem, while continuing over the fences.

Trotting-Poles with Fences at Bounce Distances
This exercise also helps the rider's position. It is performed over trotting-poles followed by fences at bounce distances about 2.75 metres (9ft) apart. (Suitable for 13.2hh ponies jumping fences at .6m or 2ft high). In this case the distances become even more critical, as the ponies should land and immediately take off again without a stride. If a long-striding pony tries to jump two fences at a time, or if a short-striding pony takes a stride between the fences, chaos will ensue. Use it, therefore, only when the ponies have worked over trotting-poles, on to gymnastic exercises, and are ready to progress. Fig. 44 shows one bounce, but further fences may be added, with the same distance between them once the original fence has been performed satisfactorily.

The distances given above are approximate. They will ultimately depend on the size of the ponies, the lengths of their strides, and the height of the fences.

Gymnastics without Trotting-Poles
These have a special value in developing or restoring confidence when jumping from the canter – though they may also be approached from the trot. They are used most effectively when giving a private lesson or a lesson with a small number of riders whose ponies have identical strides. Sometimes a ride may be split into two groups, and the distances adjusted for each group.

Equipment
A minimum of four pairs of stands and nine poles will be needed.

Positioning of Equipment
Build a small fence, and position the stands ready to build two more fences each about 6 metres away from the last. Use two pairs of stands for a third fence. At this stage do not position the stands accurately.

Method
After the ride has carried out the usual preliminary exercises and has jumped the small jump from trot and canter, build a second larger fence 6 metres (approx. 19½ft) away. This distance should be correct for ponies of 13.2hh approaching the double in a steady canter. Watch each pony jump the double carefully, and repeat the exercise until the whole ride is jumping it fluently. If necessary, adjust the distance between the fences and repeat the exercise again to check that the adjustment was satisfactory.

Then build a third fence (Fig. 45) the same distance away, but make it a staircase type, and measure to its first pole (the take-off pole). Make it larger than the other two, with the spread the same as the height.

Fig. 45 A combination of three jumps, seen from the side.

The ride should approach the fence at a steady canter, the first fence being merely a placing fence to help the ponies to arrive correctly at the second fence, which will require more effort. The third – largest – fence will need an even higher jump, but the ponies should find it easy, as the previous two fences will have regulated their balance and stride. The riders will learn to sit quietly, maintaining rhythm and impulsion.

If the distances are correct and the ponies are not rushing the approach to the placing fence, the second and third fences may be enlarged. Then, if all is well, the third fence may be raised again. In this way, ponies and riders find themselves approaching a larger fence confidently and without having to worry about arriving at the correct point for the take-off. Beware of over-facing the ponies.

Jumping-Lanes
Jumping-lanes are most useful, but unfortunately they are seldom available. Any of the previous exercises may be used in them. Because they have high fences which run along both sides of the lane, 'steering' problems are minimal.

In jumping-lanes the riders can concentrate on their positions and on the movement of their ponies. Once the riders are performing fluently over easy fences, they can carry out the exercises without reins, stirrups, saddles – or with their eyes closed – according to their ability. Take care that the work without stirrups or saddles does not cause tension and upward gripping with the calves. Do not allow the riders to hold on by the reins.

WARNINGS
1. Knowledge of distances and careful measuring are poor substitutes for the Instructor's eyes. While helping the riders, *watch the ponies carefully* as they negotiate trotting-poles and perform gymnastic exercises. If necessary, adjust the distances, and repeat the exercise with the whole ride. Every inch matters, and because distances are crucial, you must ensure that they are correct for all the ponies at each stage before progressing to the next. If this is not possible, do not continue with gymnastic jumping. If distances are wrong, the value of the exercise is lost, and an accident may well result.
2. Gradients and the state of the going affect distances. A distance which is correct in the indoor school will be far too long in a muddy field or up an incline.
3. Ponies which are tired or bored tend to trip, and may even fall. Jumping must be stopped before this stage is reached.

20 Instructing Senior Rides

With riders approaching 'B' standard and above, teaching will be more individual and specialised.

At this stage, the riders should be encouraged to work individually and to think out problems for themselves. Each horse must be worked so that he will progress in his training. With keen observation, the experienced teacher should be able to give individual help to every horse and rider.

There are two main methods of working a more senior ride, depending on numbers and the space available.

1. Riders, on the same rein and well spaced out round the manège, practise the same movement. When a rider feels that he is getting too close to the horse ahead he should make a turn or circle, rejoining the ride in an empty space, without breaking his horse's rhythm. At this stage it is important for each horse to work in a way which is best for him as an individual. When a rider feels that he or his horse are getting tired or have achieved their objective, he should walk his horse on a loose rein, off the track, until he is ready to work again. The Instructor, while watching all the members of the ride, should give individual help and advice. He should remember to change the rein at regular intervals.

2. When the ride is small in number and the horses are reasonably settled there is no need for all the riders to be on the same rein. As long as there is adequate space and a competent Instructor they may each work at their own task. They should be reminded to pass oncoming riders left hand to left hand. Later in the lesson, it may be sensible to use all the available space rather than being confined by the markers.

INSTRUCTORS SHOULD ENSURE THAT SENIOR RIDERS IN PARTICULAR:

- Are made aware of their own faults and how best to improve themselves.
- Learn to analyse the reasons for what they as individuals are doing.
- Are encouraged to feel and recognize why a movement went wrong and how to improve it.
- Practise putting their thoughts and feelings into words.
- Think towards progressive training for their horses.
- Consider whether their horses could be improved by changes in horsemastership (feeding, bedding, care of feet, etc.).

21   Working a Rider on the Lunge

Read the current *Manual of Horsemanship:* 'The Position of the Rider in the Saddle' and 'The Position of the Rider in Motion'. Also read 'Lungeing' in *Breeding, Backing and Bringing on Young Horses and Ponies.*

Purpose

To improve the position of the rider. Without the need to control the horse, the rider is able to concentrate on improving his riding. This improvement will help him to be more effective in all branches of horse-manship by:

1. Building his confidence.
2. Improving his balance.
3. Developing a supple, secure and elegant position from which the aids can be correctly and easily applied.
4. Eliminating stiffness.

These will lead to the development of 'feel' and will result in increased harmony between horse and rider.

Standard

Lungeing helps riders at all levels, provided that the Instructor is sufficiently skilled, and that the length and demands of the lesson are appropriate.

The Instructor should at all times pay attention to the following:

1. Confidence.
2. The rider's balance, especially through transitions and changes of speed. The rider should not tip forwards or backwards and should be aware of the equal distribution of weight on both seat bones.
3. Confidence, suppleness and balance are inter-dependent. Lack of confidence can create stiffness. Stiffness can disrupt balance.
4. If the rider is struggling to keep his balance, there is no point in the Instructor telling him to 'relax'. Confidence must first be restored by returning to a slower pace or even to the halt, in order to re-establish this essential balance.
5. Evidence of excess tension can be seen in all parts of the body, but it is most clearly revealed in the extremities – i.e head, hands, and feet.

Requirements
1. A suitable horse or pony which is accustomed to being used for lungeing a rider, and whose paces are regular, steady and comfortable. It is important that he responds to the commands given to him, while ignoring those given, in a different tone, to the rider.
2. An Instructor or his assistant to lunge the horse. Whoever does so must have the necessary experience and knowledge of lungeing to maintain complete control. It can be advantageous for the Instructor to be free to stand on the outside of the circle so that he can observe the rider from all sides.
3. Correct lungeing equipment, including a saddle which fits both horse and rider, and a bridle. See 'Lungeing' in *Training Young Horses* for correct equipment and how to fit it.
4. A suitable site; preferably an enclosed flat area with good going, approximately 20 to 30 metres square.

Method
1. Before the rider mounts, the horse should be worked at walk, trot and canter on both reins, until he is settled and obedient. It is usual to work first without, and later with, side reins. Secure the side reins to each other over the withers when they are not fastened to the bit.
2. When the horse is ready, bring him to a halt and unfasten the side reins. The rider should mount, adjust the stirrup leathers and take up a loose rein. The bridle reins are there in the first place to give the rider confidence. As soon as the rider is happy, they can be secured over the neck and need not be used again. But they should always be there in case of an emergency.
3. At the halt, show the rider how to rest both hands lightly on the pommel of the saddle; and how easy it is, from there, to slip the fingers under the pommel at any time if he feels insecure. This will be his emergency procedure if he loses his balance later on. *HE SHOULD NEVER HOLD ON BY THE REINS.* Re-fasten the side reins.
4. Explain the correct position.
5. At the walk, encourage the rider to feel the movement of the horse. The correct position should be maintained. Check that the rider's hips are parallel with horses' hips and that his shoulders are parallel with the horse's shoulders.
6. Do some simple loosening exercises which allow the rider to discover the freedom of riding without reins – e.g. arm-circling, one arm at a time.

7. To establish confidence the rider may have a brief period, retaining his stirrups, in rising and then in sitting trot. The easiest trot at this stage is a slow, rather idle, pace, with the horse's head low.

8. The Instructor must use his discretion in deciding what the next stage will be. With some riders, further work with stirrups will be required. In general, some work without stirrups is beneficial. Depending on the rider's standard and fitness, the lesson may contain a mixture of:
   - ☐ Transitions.
   - ☐ Variations in pace and speed.
   - ☐ Exercises.

9. Only advanced riders on experienced lunge horses should be allowed to canter.

10. Work on the lunge is strenuous and should be broken up by frequent periods of rest and discussion. A total of ten minutes' work may be too much for those unaccustomed to riding a lunged horse.

11. During periods of rest, and at the end of the lesson, encourage the rider to stretch and then shake out any stiffness which has crept into his body.

12. Remember to work equally on both reins.

13. Unfasten the side reins from the bit before the rider dismounts.

NOTE: The Instructor should be alert to the rider's position at all times, making helpful comments and corrections.

Exercises

These will usually be performed at the walk.

Chapter 8 (page 48) deals with physical exercises. Those described in 'A few exercises used for specific purposes' are all suitable for the rider on the lunge. As the rider is not controlling the horse and need not hold the reins, he is free to perform a greater variety of exercises, especially with his upper body. Some of these are:

1. Slowly moving the head, describing with the nose a horizontal figure-of-eight (the sign of infinity).
2. Individual arm-circling, forwards, upwards and round.
3. Both arms circling, as above, or swinging forward and backwards.
4. Position of the hands:
   (a) Holding the saddle.
   (b) Straight down by the horse's sides.
   (c) Arms outstretched sideways, palms uppermost.
   (d) Hands on the head, elbows in line with shoulders.
   (e) Hands in riding position.

5. Arms to the side and circling individually forwards, upwards and across, at the same time twisting the trunk to touch the point of the horse's opposite hip with the fingers.
6. Arms to the side and a little to the rear, without body movement, bringing the heels up alternately to touch the hands.
7. Raising one arm then bending down to touch the toe on the same side.
8. Knee and thigh taken sideways off the saddle (short periods only).

Perhaps the most useful exercise to be performed by the rider at the halt or walk is stretching both legs slowly down and a little backward out to the side from the hip joint, then allowing them to return to the saddle, keeping the knees low on the saddle flap. This will help to improve the rider's leg position, with the thigh flat against the saddle.

The Instructor must decide when the rider is too relaxed or too tense, and use suitable exercises to help him. He should take care that problems such as upward gripping with the thighs and calves, or tension in other places, do not result from doing work which is too difficult for the rider at that stage. Remember that as the pace increases the same exercises become more difficult.

THE MORE ADVANCED RIDER will be able to have a longer lesson, but he should still have frequent periods of physical rest at the walk, during which discussion may be useful. Only when his position is basically correct will he be able to stay in balance. If for any reason he becomes insecure and is unable to regain his balance, the horse should be brought back to walk.

Riders working for the 'A' test should be able to maintain a supple and independent position on the lunge, with the hands in the riding position.

Appendix

The Syllabus of Instruction for The Pony Club

This syllabus has been produced to help Instructors to cover all the ground necessary for the various standards. When asked to take a ride, an Instructor should be told at which stage the ride is working. He will then know what to teach.

The whole course has been divided into stages, each of which corresponds approximately to a year's instruction. At the end of certain stages, efficiency tests should be taken by those who are considered up to standard.

The items on the test cards shown under 'Other Instruction' cover the *Riding and Road Safety Test* and, in the later stages, essential practical and theoretical knowledge, without which it is impossible to become a good horseman and horsemaster, or to pass the higher standards.

Some members progress faster than others. While these should not be held back, it is important that they should follow the sequence and not miss any part of the syllabus. It must be realised that some members attend more rallies than others. When promoting members to a higher stage care must be taken that they are up to the standard in riding and horsemastership, both in theory and practice.

The ages mentioned in the syllabus are a guide and should not be compulsory. Chief Instructors must use their own discretion, especially when dealing with riders who join The Pony Club at a later age.

Achievement Badges cover the following; Bandaging and Rugs; First Aid (Equine); Handling and Grooming; Loading; Mucking Out; Points of the Horse: Saddlery; Shoeing; Bird Watching; Farming; Flowers; Map Reading; Poisonous Plants; Trees; Wildlife; Working Dogs; Road Sense; First Aid (Human); British Native Breeds (Horses and Ponies). It is suggested that they should be used in conjunction with the various standards.

It is essential to stress the importance of continuous repetition and revision.

STAGES 1 AND 2
Towards D Test. Ages approx. 6 to 9 years

RIDING
Mounting and dismounting and training the pony to stand.
Reasonably correct position in the saddle.
Holding single reins.
Walk, trot and turn, off the leading-rein.
Games. Simple balancing exercises at halt.

HORSEMASTERSHIP
How to approach and handle a pony.
Importance of the voice.
Correct way to give an apple or carrot.
Catch a pony and put on a headcollar or halter.
Lead and turn a pony in hand at walk.
Points, colours and markings.
Name parts of the saddle and bridle.

OTHER INSTRUCTION
How to ride along and cross a road.
How to say 'Thank you' to motorists.
Know that it is safer to ride on the road accompanied by a
    responsible adult.

STAGE 3
Preparation for D Test. Ages 8 to 9 years

RIDING
Revise previous stages.
Turnout of pony and rider. How to hold a whip.
Walk without stirrups. Position at the trot.
Use of the aids to increase and decrease pace,
    and importance of the voice while riding.
Work in open at walk and trot.
Walk away from other ponies.
Games and balancing exercises.

HORSEMASTERSHIP
Revise previous stages.
Basic needs of the pony in summer and winter.
Picking up the feet.
Use of the hoof-pick.
Trot a pony in hand.
Daily care of the pony at grass.
Tie up pony and haynet.
Names and uses of essential grooming kit.

OTHER INSTRUCTION
Revise previous stages.
Know which side of the road to lead or ride.
Hand signals (knowledge and practice).
Safety precautions before leading pony on to a road.
Introduce a pony, first to stationary, and later to moving vehicles.
Insist on obedience when on the road.
Know what causes a pony to slip or shy.

Check that the current 'D' Standard syllabus has been covered.

The recommended minimum age for taking 'D' Standard Test is 8 or 9 years.

STAGE 4
Preparation for D+ Test. Ages 9 to 11 years

RIDING
Revise previous stages.
Balance exercises at walk.
Alter stirrups when mounted.
Tighten and loosen girth when mounted.
Move freely forward at walk and trot.
Simple turns and circles at walk and trot.
Position and aids for canter.
Walk on a loose rein and shorten the reins.
Ride up and down hills.
Jumping position.
Jump very small fences.
Games.

HORSEMASTERSHIP
Revise previous stages.
Early lessons in indications of health in the pony, and dosing for worms.
Recognize obvious lameness.
Preparation of a field for a pony at grass.
Care and cleaning of saddlery.
Use of stable tools to muck out.
Recognize New Zealand rugs, sweat rugs and night rugs.
Put on a saddle and bridle.

OTHER INSTRUCTION
Revise previous stages.
Moving off down the road.
Left and right turns.
Overtaking stationary vehicles.
Know police signals and road signs.
How to ride on the road in company.
Practise riding past hazards (tractors etc.) in a safe place.
Early lessons on countryside lore and hunting.

Check that the current 'D+' Standard syllabus has been covered.

The recommended minimum age for taking D+ Test is 10 years.

'D+' is an official but optional test half-way between 'D' and 'C' standards.

STAGE 5
Preparation for C Test. Ages 10 to 12 years

RIDING

Revise previous stages.

Trot for short period without stirrups.

Walk and trot on a loose rein.

Hold the reins in one hand.

Rising trot on either diagonal and change of diagonal.

Be aware of and apply correct aids.

Canter on named leg on circle.

Sequence of legs at all paces.

Position at gallop.

Jump small fences from trot and canter.

Jump small ditches.

Riders should be insisting that pony behaves with good manners: e.g. quiet with other ponies, traffic, dogs, hunting whip, polo stick, etc. Must stand when required.

Games and vaulting.

HORSEMASTERSHIP

Revise previous stages.

Care of the pony working off grass at all times of year.

Elementary feeding, watering, and cleanliness.

Measuring and height of pony.

Signs that pony needs the farrier.

What to look for in a newly shod foot.

Treatment of minor wounds and illness.

Necessary protection against tetanus and 'flu.

Roll up and put on travelling bandages and tail bandages.

Put on a rug, a roller and a New Zealand rug.

Understand the importance and means of protecting the legs while travelling.

Taking pony into and out of a horse box or trailer.

OTHER INSTRUCTION

Revise previous stages.

The law regarding riding on verges and footpaths.

Riding and leading at dusk or in poor visibility.

Riding on slippery roads.

Riding in the countryside on bridle paths and across farm land.

Know the contents of the current *Riding and Roadcraft* booklet.

Practise the theoretical and practical parts of the *Riding and Road Safety Test*.

Check that the current 'C' standard syllabus has been covered.

The recommended minimum age for taking 'C' Standard Test and the Riding and Road Safety Test is 11 or 12 years.

Before being awarded the 'C' Test Certificate, candidates <u>must</u> have attained the Riding and Road Safety Achievement Badge. After 'C' but before 'B' Members must pass either the BHS Road Safety Test or the Pony Club Road Safety Test.

STAGE 6
Towards C+ Test. Ages 11 to 13 years

RIDING
Revise previous stages.
Mount and dismount on either side.
Balance exercises at halt, walk and trot.
Be aware of and apply correct aids.
Work towards feeling movement of pony's legs.
The importance of contact.
Pony should be accepting and responding to aids and working towards better balance.
Tempo and rhythm.
Turns and circles, theory and practice.
Halt and salute.
Quarter turn on the forehand from halt.
Canter on a loose rein.
Ride up and down steep hills.
The correct approach when jumping. Jump a course of small fences including double jumps.
Games.

HORSEMASTERSHIP
Revise previous stages.
Practical care of a pony working off grass, or partially stabled (combined system).
Procedure on return from hunting or a strenuous day out.
Make a bran mash.
Recognise when a pony is lame, sick, or in poor condition.
Be aware that a knowledgeable person should periodically check the pony's mouth for sharp teeth and other problems.
Groom a pony effectively; strap; make a wisp.
Fit saddles, bridles, and martingales.
Elementary knowledge of bits, their actions and uses.
Care and storage of rugs and saddlery.

OTHER INSTRUCTION
How to behave out hunting and cub-hunting.
Open gates with hand or whip.
Preparations for a day's hunting or a competition.
How to give a leg-up.
How to show a pony.
Ride with regard to others on the roads and in the country.
Have a knowledge of pace and distance.

STAGE 7
Preparation for C+ Test. Ages 12 to 14 years

RIDING
Revise previous stages.
Exercises to develop independent position.

Understand balance. Feel when a horse loses balance.
Basic paces and transitions.
Half turn on forehand from halt.
Change of leg at canter through trot.
Ride with two pairs of reins.
Jump small fences with and without reins and stirrups (in safety).
Jump going up and down hills and over ditches
Know how and when to gallop.
Deal with run-outs and refusals. Correct use of whip.
Games.

HORSEMASTERSHIP
Revise previous stages.
Principles of watering, feeding and exercising and their practical
    application to the stabled horse and the pony working off grass.
Know and recognize the usual items of forage and its quality. The use,
    if necessary, of vitamin and mineral supplements.
Know the parts of a foot and have some knowledge of its structure.
Name the farrier's tools.
Describe a hunter shoe.
Know the usual types of bedding and how to use them.
Rug up with all usual types of rugs and with a blanket.
Put on boots and working bandages.
Carry out prescribed treatment of wounds, ailments and lameness.
How to prepare a pony for travelling, and what to feed on the journey.

OTHER INSTRUCTION
How to ride through water.
Walk cross-country and show-jumping courses intelligently.
Ride in junior or novice competitions.
Ride sensibly on the roads and in the country, alone or in company.
Have consideration for others riding in the group and for people on
    foot.

Check that the current 'C+' Standard syllabus has been covered.

The recommended age for taking the 'C+' Standard Test is 14 years.
'C+' is an official but optional test half-way between 'C' and 'B' standards.

STAGE 8
Towards B Test. Ages 13 to 15 years

RIDING
Revise previous stages.
Work on developing a secure, independent position at all paces.
Understand and apply correct aids at all times.
Transitions, turns, circles, serpentines (at trot).
Quarter-pirouette at walk. Rein-back.

Ride other members' horses and be able to discuss them.
Ride with the reins in either hand.
Know the usual riding school drill.
Ride in a double bridle.
Jump a variety of fences and ditches at trot and canter.

HORSEMASTERSHIP
Revise previous stages.
Grooming, feeding, and exercising a corn-fed stabled horse. Wash mane,
    tail and sheath. Plait and trim; pull manes and tails.
Tempt a shy feeder to eat.
Good and bad points of conformation. Movement and action of a horse.
Action of the three basic types of bit. How they should fit the horse.
Care and storage of rugs and saddlery, inspection for soundness, and
organisation of tack room.

OTHER INSTRUCTION
Plan exercising of horses and ponies, using appropriate paces and
    distance.
Know routes of local bridal paths and help to keep them open by riding
    down them sensibly.

STAGE 9
Preparation for test B Test. Ages 14 to 17 years
RIDING
Revise previous stages.
Work on position at all paces.
Understand the importance of straightness and impulsion.
Ride the usual school movements in the manège.
Achieve some shortening (working towards collection) and lengthening
    of strides.
leg yielding in walk and trot.
Half-pirouette at walk.
Practise riding different horses.
How to show off a horse.
Jump a course of small show jumps. Understand importance of balance,
    rhythm and impulsion.
Jump up and down hill and across a slope.
Jump 'drops', slipping reins if necessary. Be able to recover reins
    correctly.
Ride with a knowledge of pace and balance at cross-country speed.

HORSEMASTERSHIP
Revise previous stages.
Practical care of the stabled horse.
Bringing a horse up from grass; conditioning for hunting or hard work;
    roughing off and turning out to grass.
Care of the stabled horse after hunting or a strenuous day out.
Hot and cold shoeing; how the farrier removes the shoes, prepares the
    foot and re-shoes a horse.
Know the different types of common shoe.

Studs and their uses.

Some knowledge of ageing teeth.

Recognize when a horse is lame, ill or in poor condition; know the common cause of these problems.

Some knowledge of the stable construstion, ventilation, light, drainage, shelter, and warmth.

Prepare a horse for travel and be capable of inspecting, loading and unloading a horse into or out of a box or trailer.

OTHER INSTRUCTION
Practical experience of horse trials, hunting or long-distance riding.

Practical experience of feeding, using basic and ready-mixed feed.

Check that the current 'B' Standard syllabus has been covered.

The recommended minimum age for taking the 'B' Standard Test is 15 or 16 years. Members must be 14 years or over to take the Test.

STAGE 10
Towards A Test. Ages 16 to 19

RIDING
Revise previous stages.

Work on position.

Improve co-ordination of leg and hand.

Ride accurate school movements.

Leg-yielding.

Ride different horses in various stages of training, on the flat and over fences.

Analyse their problems. Work towards improving them.

Be able to explain how horse is working on the flat and over fences. Discuss schooling plans.

Understand use of trotting-poles and gymnastic jumping.

HORSEMASTERSHIP
Revise previous stages.

Daily routine of the stable yard.

Check horses first thing in morning and last thing at night.

Conformation and accurate description of a horse.

Lead a horse on the near and off side for showing or vet's inspection.

Methods of holding a horse still for treatment or clipping.

Types of clip and when used.

Deal with a cast horse.

Cook horse-feed correctly (linseed, barley and oats).

Symptoms of exhaustion, and nursing the exhausted horse.

Detection of heat and swelling in horse's legs.

Diseases and ailments of the foot.

Taking temperature, pulse and respiration.

Examination of saddlery for soundness.

Types of saddlery, their uses and fitting.

OTHER INSTRUCTION
Horse and pony breeds and their characteristics.
Societies connected with the welfare of horses and ponies.
Grassland management.
Lunge a horse for exercise; the reasons for lungeing.
Go on a basic Instructor's course.
Care and handling of foals and young horses and ponies.
First aid for riders.
Security for horses, property and equipment.
Insurance.

STAGE 11
Preparation for A Test. Ages 17 to 21

RIDING
Revise previous stages.
Work to achieve a secure, independent position.
Ride effectively and with 'feel'.
Carry out the basic training of a young horse, and correct faults in the
    older horse.
Gain experience in the use of the double bridle when riding.
Understand 'acceptance of the bit' and 'engagement of the hind-
    quarters'.
Plan and ride a sequence of school movements in a logical order. Explain
    correct aids.
Shoulder-in.
Ride across country with determination and confidence, jumping
    various fences at appropriate speeds.
Plan and ride a show-jumping round, maintaining balance, rhythm and
    impulsion.
Use trotting-poles and fences at related distances correctly.

HORSEMASTERSHIP
Revise previous stages.
Plan the running of a stable yard and be able to take sole charge for a
    limited period.
The skeletal and muscular systems and their effect on the performance
and movement of the horse.
The circulatory system. Dealing with severe bleeding.
The respiratory system. Respiratory diseases and unsoundness.
The welfare of the corn-fed stabled horse and the horse at grass.
Maintaining or improving condition.
Stable tricks and vices.
Handling difficult horses in and out of the stable.
Recognize and treat common injuries and ailments.
Sick nursing.
Seats of lameness: how to feel for them.
Care of horse's teeth. Examination for sharp or wolf teeth; ageing.
Clipping and care of the clipping machine.

Planning a stable yard; fire precautions; organisation of feed store, hay barn and muck-heap.
Precautions against contagion and infection.

OTHER INSTRUCTION
Have a knowledge of vetting horses for purchase.
Ride and lead with lead horse on either side.
Prepare, exercise and put away two horses (ride and lead) without help.
Basic training of the young horse or pony in theory and practice.
Lungeing a young horse for training; backing; preliminary schooling.
Preparation and safety of horse-box or trailer.

Mares and Foals
Selection of brood mare and of stallion.
Choice of service date. Basic outline of covering programme.
Foaling environments, facilities and equipment; selection, preparations and procedures.
Care of the in-foal mare, including feeding, worming and testing routines.
Precautionary measures, e.g. tetanus and influenza.
Know when to call the veterinary surgeon.
Signs of mare about to foal.
What to watch out for when mare is foaling.
Deciding factors on whether to return mare to stud; procedures then necessary.
Transporting mares and foals.
Weaning: when and how.
Gelding colts: advantages and disadvantages.

Check that current 'A' Horse and Pony Care syllabus and/or 'A' Riding Syllabus have been covered.

Test for 'A' Standard should be taken at ages 17 to 21 years. Candidates must be 17 years or over. Before attempting the 'A' Horse and Pony Care Standard Test the 'B' Standard Certificate must be held. Before taking 'A' Riding Test the 'A' Horse and Pony Care Test must be passed.

STAGE 12
Having passed 'A' Test Standard

Members who reach stage 12 have passed the test for 'A' Standard, which is the highest award of the Pony Club. These young people have thus proved considerable ability, and are now ready to move ahead in their chosen equestrian fields, widening their experience and increasing their knowledge. It is hoped that, at convenient times in the future, they will wish to put back, as instructors or officials, some of the knowledge and fun which was provided for them in the Pony Club.

Index

* Numbers in italics refer to page numbers of diagrams.